BOOK 1

GETTING ALONG: ENGLISH GRAMMAR AND WRITING

DONNA BRINTON
REGINA NEUMAN
UCLA

Photography by JAMES HEATON

Selected illustrations by SARA ARDITTI

PRENTICE-HALL, INC.
Englewood Cliffs, New Jersey 07632

Library of Congress Cataloging in Publication Data

Brinton, Donna M.   (date)
  Getting along.

  Includes indexes.
    1. English language—Text-books for foreigners.
2. English language—Grammar.   I. Neuman,
Regina A.   II. Title.
PE1128.B675   428.2'4   81–19246
ISBN   0–13–354456–7 (bk. 1)   AACR2
ISBN   0–13–354464–8 (bk. 2)

© 1982 by Prentice-Hall, Inc., Englewood Cliffs, N.J. 07632

Printed in the United States of America

10 9 8 7 6 5 4 3 2 1

Editorial/production supervision
    and interior design by Barbara Alexander
Art production by Charles Pelletreau
Cover design by Wanda Lubelska
Manufacturing buyer: Harry P. Baisley
Graphic design and layout
    by Donna Brinton and Regina Neuman
Initial art concepts by
    Linda Chan, Susan Stern,
    Behrouz Azarvand, and Kyuji Nakamura

ISBN 0-13-354456-7

Prentice-Hall International, Inc., *London*
Prentice-Hall of Australia Pty. Limited, *Sydney*
Prentice-Hall of Canada, Ltd., *Toronto*
Prentice-Hall of India Private Limited, *New Delhi*
Prentice-Hall of Japan, Inc., *Tokyo*
Prentice-Hall of Southeast Asia Pte. Ltd., *Singapore*
Whitehall Books Limited, *Wellington, New Zealand*

CONTENTS

CHAPTER
three

AT THE HOUSING OFFICE   *51*

CHAPTER
four

DECIDING TO LIVE TOGETHER   *75*

CHAPTER
five

LET'S HAVE COFFEE   *105*

CHAPTER
six

LOOKING FOR AN APARTMENT   *139*

CHAPTER
seven

AT THE PIER   *165*

CHAPTER
eight

MEETING THE LANDLORD   *193*

CHAPTER
nine

MOVING DAY *223*

CHAPTER
ten

PEACE CONFERENCE *251*

INDEX *275*

TO THE TEACHER

INTRODUCTION

Getting Along is a beginning-level grammar and writing text which was created to fill the needs of adult second language learners of English in an academic or pre-academic setting. As such, it is especially suited for those students who are university bound as well as for the many working professionals who require a high level of competency in English. The text is ideal for any highly-motivated student: It offers a comprehensive introduction to the English language for the beginning-level student, and a challenging review of the basics of the English language for slightly more advanced learners.

The text has been extensively classroom tested with students from virtually every major language background at both the community college and university levels. We feel that *Getting Along* can be used with equal success at universities, state and community colleges, and in any intensive language program, provided the students are academically oriented. Depending on the students' initial proficiency level and on the quantity of supplementary materials or classroom activities the teacher chooses to use in the program, we estimate that the two volumes of *Getting Along* will require 150–200 hours of classroom time.

THE CONTEXT

Getting Along presents all grammar structures within the context of a single, modern-day story. The central episode of each chapter, presented in an introductory dialogue, reflects topics of universal concern which are of special interest to the student who is in the process of adjusting to a new culture. The grammatical explanations following the dialogue refer back to the chapter's main episode in order to exemplify the grammatical point under discussion.

In addition to the main event of each chapter, many supplementary episodes involving the characters are revealed throughout the course of the exercises. Students are motivated to probe into the various levels of exercises in order to discover this additional information about the characters and events— thereby gaining valuable additional language practice.

The text's situational realism is heightened by the use of photographs which animate the personalities of the characters as well as add validity to the context. As a result, students feel that they are reading about *real* individuals, and they are able to relate the experiences of these characters to their own daily lives.

THE APPROACH

Our philosophy toward the teaching of structure is twofold: to emphasize the communicative nature of any given linguistic item and to focus on English structure as an integrated part of the larger writing context. To this end, we have clustered the syntactic structures presented in each chapter around the specific situations and semantic notions of the chapter-initial dialogues. These situations and notions are further exploited in the exercise materials, which develop and reinforce the students' command of the language. In the controlled and free paragraph-writing exercises at the end of each chapter, students are required to *use* the structures that have just been presented in contexts from the text as well as in expositions based on the students' own experiences. The students are thus guided into composition writing at an early level.

The text, therefore, does *not* focus on linguistic structures in isolation. Instead, *Getting Along* emphasizes the communicative and expository function of linguistic structures. It is our belief that by teaching students to express their ideas orally, and by making organized paragraph writing a primary aim even at this elementary level of language instruction, we can better serve the needs of the types of students this text is intended to serve.

ORGANIZATION

Each chapter of the text is organized in the following manner. A short dialogue incorporating the structural items to be covered serves as an introduction. We have attempted to use natural colloquial speech in these dialogues and to choose those contexts which the foreign student typically encounters in the second language environment, such as renting an apartment, dealing with the landlord, buying a car, and so on.

Following the dialogue in each chapter are a series of thorough grammar explanations, sequenced to facilitate the students' acquisition of the language. These explanations reinforce classroom explanation and are part of a total program aimed at improving the students' skills in using the language. They are not intended to teach abstract rules of grammar, but rather to encourage correct, meaningful application of these—both in the controlled and free composition exercises and in the students' oral use of the language. For students preferring a less-detailed approach to English structure, we have included numerous charts which graphically present the most essential grammatical items. We must caution that the explanations contained in the text are not meant to substitute for teacher explanation, but rather to augment the foundation laid during the in-class presentation and to serve both the student and the teacher as a valuable reference source.

Finally, a particularly innovative feature of this text is the wealth of exercises following the core of each chapter. These are divided into three levels: The A-level exercises usually require students to fill in correct syntactic forms in the blanks provided; B-level exercises involve slightly more creative, sentence-writing activities; and C-level exercises consist of controlled and guided paragraph writing based on the grammatical points presented in each chapter. As such, the text is ideally suited for the type of elementary-level program (e.g., any intensive language program) in which the student population is of a diverse nature—both in terms of language background and language proficiency.

HOW TO USE *GETTING ALONG*

Getting Along offers an ideal basis for classroom activities.

Dialogues: We suggest that the teacher introduce the chapter-initial dialogue in class, before the students study it on their own. Unfamiliar vocabulary should be presented and discussed. The students can either be assigned parts and the dialogue read aloud in class, or they can be asked to read over the dialogue at home. Once the students have had a chance to read the dialogue alone, the instructor asks oral comprehension questions and discusses the situation presented in the chapter. Students are then encouraged to discuss implications of the situation presented, how they feel about the situation in the context of the United States culture, and how the situation would be handled in their native cultures.

Grammar Component: The presentation of structure will no doubt vary from teacher to teacher, and of course from structure to structure. We strongly suggest that a combination of inductive and deductive approaches toward the teaching of structure be used, and that the explanations in the text itself be used for student reference at home, rather than as an in-class tool. The sentences at the beginning of each major grammar heading (written on the blackboard or on an overhead transparency) can serve as useful examples for analysis and rule formation. However, whenever possible we encourage teachers to provide a context for the structure being taught through the use of pictures, audio recordings, games, and the like. We have found it particularly effective to individualize the lesson by using our own experiences and those of our students. The increased interest level of the students when they are the subjects of the language lesson speaks strongly for this approach. To exemplify: In Chapter Four, Book 2, the initial chapter dialogue about Bill's bad habits sets the context for the presentation of conditional structures used in making promises or resolutions. Teachers could individualize this context by telling students about their own bad habits, and asking students what promises or resolutions they should make to their spouses, friends, etc. to remedy the situation. The sentences elicited from students can then be written on the board, corrected, and analyzed. Follow-up activities might involve having students work in pairs or small groups discussing their own bad habits, writing up their own resolutions and subsequently presenting these orally to the class.

The above example can serve as a model for the instructor's grammar presentations. To summarize, the presentations should be relevant to the students' experiences and environment, but similar in format to the presentations used in the text.

Exercises: Procedures used with the exercises will also vary immensely from teacher to teacher. The three levels of exercises lend themselves to individualization of instruction: With slower learners or groups of learners, the instructor may wish to assign only A- or B-level exercises; the teacher desiring a very thorough introduction to the English language may wish to assign all levels of exercises to all students. Finally, instructors with advanced learners or groups of learners may be more selective in their choice of exercises and assign only those which they feel to be more challenging. A common denominator to all of the above, however, is the unchanging rule that students should never be required to complete exercises until the instructor is certain that they have had the necessary practice in the classroom and that the exercise is totally within their range of competency.

CONCLUSION

It is our sincere wish that you and your students find these materials relevant and enjoyable to use. We wrote them in the spirit of trying to facilitate the job of teaching ESL at this level. We welcome any comments you might have concerning your experiences with the text.

DONNA M. BRINTON

REGINA A. NEUMAN

Los Angeles, California

ACKNOWLEDGMENTS

In the course of writing our text, we had the great fortune to be assisted, encouraged, and enlightened by family, friends, and colleagues. We thank them all.

We are extremely grateful to Marianne Celce-Murcia and Laurel Brinton for their extensive linguistic editing offered at the initial stages of our project. Their many critical comments were indispensable in the creation of these materials. As well, we wish to thank Miguel Aparicio for his comments concerning the content of the exercises and the sequencing of grammatical items, and Ruth Schweitzer whose eye for detail caught many of the inconsistencies in the original manuscript.

For his great patience and skill and for the hours of hard work he spent on location and in the dark room in the interest of providing us with the photographs used throughout this text, we are extremely grateful to Jim Heaton. His promptness and willingness to meet unreasonable deadlines were always appreciated, as were the many suggestions he made for improving the style and content of the materials.

We would like to express special gratitude to our cast of characters for the many hours spent under duress during our lengthy photographic sessions. Their extreme cooperation and patience enabled us to complete the project as originally envisioned. We would also like to thank the supporting cast who, while giving us fewer hours of their time, were equally cooperative.

Furthermore, we are thankful to Linda Chan, Sara Arditti, Kyuji Nakamura, Susan Stern and Behrouz Azarvand for the art work which appeared in the prepublication materials. These illustrations enabled us to classroom test the materials and provided ideas and inspiration for much of the art work contained in the published text. We owe an additional thanks to Behrouz Azarvand for the many long hours he devoted toward the development of the materials, and for his willingness to share with us his many talents.

We are grateful to the faculty and staff at the American Language Center, UCLA Extension Division, and Marymount Palos Verdes College for allowing us to use these materials in their beginning-level ESL classes. We appreciate the comments and criticism we received from both the teachers and students involved in the classroom testing procedure.

Finally, we wish to express gratitude to Mr. and Mrs. R. K. Brinton and to the countless others who encouraged us in our attempt to publish these materials. We particularly thank Mr. and Mrs. Benjamin Neuman for their generosity and hospitality during the hours we spent writing and assembling the manuscript. Additionally, we wish to thank them for their invaluable advice and their willingness to help us with a multitude of tasks.

CAST
OF CHARACTERS

Main Characters (in order of appearance):

Darlene Peterson	Regina Neuman	Bill Starsky	James Brown
Chrissy Peterson	Christine Brinton	Meg Bernstein	Barbara Jaffe
Jonathan Moscowitz	John Hayes	Adrienne Hamilton	Cherry Campbell
Gary Chapman	James Heaton	Mr. Garvey	Benjamin Neuman

Supporting Characters (in order of appearance):

Bev	Donna Brinton	Carol & George	Frances and Takis Hinofotis
Ms. Olson	Edie Olson	Jeff	Fereidoun Navi
Susie	Maureen Secord	Mrs. Bernstein	Anne Neuman

INTRODUCTIONS

This is Darlene. She is 32 years old. She's a student at the university. She's from Pennsylvania.

This is Chrissy. She's seven. She's in the 2nd grade. She's from Pennsylvania. Darlene is Chrissy's mother.

This is Jonathan. He's 31 years old. He's a graduate student. He's from Massachusetts.

This is Gary. He's 37. He's from Oregon. He's not a student. He's a 3rd grade teacher. He and Jonathan are friends.

This is Bill. He's from California. Bill isn't a student. He's a tennis teacher. He's 28 years old.

This is Meg. She's from Illinois. She's a student. She's 26 years old.

NOUNS

	COMMON COUNT NOUNS		PROPER NOUNS
	SINGULAR	PLURAL	
H U M A N	teacher mother student	teachers mothers students	Meg Darlene Jonathan Gary Chrissy
N O N H U M A N	house city state table	houses cities states tables	California San Diego Oregon Pennsylvania Los Angeles Canada Germany

Notes

A. Noun classes: Nouns can be common or proper, count or mass.

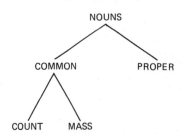

B. Common nouns: Common nouns indicate general categories or classes of things.

> **examples**   Bill is a *teacher*.
> > (common noun)
>
> New York is a large *city*.
> > (common noun)

1. Common nouns can be count or mass.
   a. Count nouns: These nouns have singular and plural forms.

   > **examples**   Bill is a tennis *teacher*.
   > > (singular count noun)
   >
   > Bill and Gary are *teachers*.
   > > (plural count noun)

   b. Mass nouns: We do not use a plural form with these nouns. They cannot be counted.

   > **examples**   The *air* is cool in the evening.
   > > (mass noun)
   >
   > The *traffic* is heavy.
   > > (mass noun)

2. Proper nouns: Proper nouns include names of people, places, days, months, holidays, nationalities, etc. Proper nouns begin with capital letters.

COMMON	PROPER
teacher	Gary
day	Monday
country	France
city	Boston

> **examples**   *Gary* is a *teacher*.
> > (proper (common
> >   noun)   noun)
>
> *Boston* is a *city*.
> > (proper   (common
> >   noun)   noun)
>
> *Harvard* is a *university*.
> > (proper   (common noun)
> >   noun)

C. Noun phrases: A noun phrase is a single noun or a group of words that contain a noun. The noun is the most important word in the phrase.
   1. A noun phrase frequently consists of a noun and an article (A, AN, or THE).

   > **examples**   Is there *a* telephone near here?
   > > (article)
   >
   > *The* campus is large.
   > > (article)

   2. A noun phrase can include one or more adjectives.

   > **examples**   The *tall   man* is Gary.
   > > (adj.) (noun)
   >
   > The *old brick   building* is Dodd Hall.
   > > (adjectives) (noun)

   3. A noun phrase can include a noun compound.

   > **examples**   Darlene is a *graduate student*.
   > > (noun compound)
   >
   > Bill is a *tennis teacher*.
   > > (noun compound)

4. Numbers frequently occur in noun phrases.
   a. When the number is more than one, the noun is plural.

   > **examples**   Chrissy is seven year*s* old.
   >   There are six student*s* in line.

D. Regular noun plurals
   1. Spelling rules
      a. Add -ES to nouns ending in -O, -S, -SS, -SH, -CH, -TCH, -Z, and -X.

	SINGULAR NOUN FORM	PLURAL NOUN FORM
-O	tomato	tomato*es*
-S	bus	bus*es*
-SS	glass	glass*es*
-SH	eyelash	eyelash*es*
-CH	lunch	lunch*es*
-TCH	match	mat*ches*
-Z	quiz	qui*zzes*
-X	fox	fox*es*

   b. When a noun ends in a consonant plus -Y, the -Y changes to -I before -ES to form the plural.

CONSONANT + Y		VOWEL + Y	
city	cit*ies*	tray	tra*ys*
library	librar*ies*	boy	bo*ys*
university	universit*ies*	day	da*ys*

(BUT)

   c. Add -S to all other regular nouns.

SINGULAR	PLURAL
student	student*s*
teacher	teacher*s*
year	year*s*

2. Pronunciation rules: There are three ways to pronounce endings of plural nouns.
   a. The plural ending is pronounced like /ɪz/ after a sibilant or "hissing" sound. The sibilant sounds in English are represented by the letters CE, S, SE, SS, SH, CH, TCH, DG, Z, and X.
   b. The plural ending is pronounced like /s/ after all other voiceless sounds. A voiceless sound is produced without the vocal chords vibrating.
   c. The plural ending is pronounced like /z/ after all voiced consonants and all vowels. A voiced sound is produced with the vocal chords vibrating.

PRONUNCIATION OF PLURAL ENDINGS		
/s/	*/z/*	*/ɪz/*
student*s*	pe*ns*	bus*es*
wee*ks*	teacher*s*	hous*es*
ta*pes*	roo*ms*	box*es*
brie*fs*	buildi*ngs*	mat*ches*
mon*ths*	da*ys*	class*es*

E. Some noun plural forms are irregular.

examples   Meg is a *woman.*
(singular form)
Meg and Darlene are *women.*
(plural form)

IRREGULAR NOUN PLURALS	
Singular	Plural
child	children
woman	women
tooth	teeth

Cardinal Numbers: 1–21

THE PRESENT TENSE OF THE VERB *BE:* STATEMENT FORM

	PRESENT TENSE FORMS OF THE VERB BE				
S I N G U L A R	I	am	not		from Pennsylvania.
	I	am			from California.
	I	am		a	teacher.
	I	am	not	a	student.
	You	are		a	student.
	You	are	not	the	teacher.
	He	is			37 years old.
	She	is	not	a	tennis teacher.
	It	is		a	large university.
	It	is	not		small.
P L U R A L	We	are			graduate students.
	We	are	not		undergraduate students.
	You	are			graduate students.
	You	are	not		teachers.
	They	are			in line.
	They	are	not		at home.

Notes

A. Form: The verb BE is an irregular verb.
B. Negative statements: BE + NOT

C. Use
1. Place and origin

    examples   We are *in line.*
    They are not *at home.*
    I am *from Egypt.*
    She is *from France.*

2. Occupation: Use A or AN with an occupation if you are talking about one person.

    examples   I am *a teacher.*
    They are *students.*

3. Identification: BE + _____
                  (noun phrase)
    examples   Darlene is *a mother.*
                      (noun phrase)
    Gary is *a tall man.*
              (noun phrase)

4. Description: BE + _____
                    (adjective)
    examples   He is *tall.*
              (adjective)
    She is *hungry.*
              (adjective)

5. Age

examples How old $\left\{ \begin{array}{l} \text{are you} \\ \text{is he} \\ \text{are they} \end{array} \right\}$? I am 23 years old.
He is 28.
They are 32.

SUBJECT PRONOUNS

	NOUNS	SUBJECT PRONOUNS
S I N G U L A R	(speaker)	I
	(listener)	you
	Bill the student	he
	Darlene the student	she
	the house	it
P L U R A L	Bill and I Meg and I Bill, Meg, and I	we
	you and Bill you and Darlene you, Bill, and Darlene	you
	Meg and Chrissy Jonathan and Gary Meg, Gary, and Bill the students the houses	they

Notes

A. Use a subject pronoun in place of a noun in the subject position.

examples *Meg* is from Chicago.   *Bill, Meg, and I* are students.
She is from Chicago.   *We* are students.

Bill is from San Diego.
He is from San Diego.

B. Pronoun Forms
  1. Third person singular form
    a. $\left\{ \begin{array}{l} \text{HE} \\ \text{SHE} \end{array} \right\}$: Use the pronouns HE and SHE for animate singular nouns. SHE refers to females. HE refers to males.

examples *The student* is from San Diego.   *The student* is from Chicago.
(Bill)   (Meg)
He is from San Diego.   *She* is from Chicago.

    b. IT: Use the pronoun IT for inanimate singular nouns. The pronoun IT is never omitted in English.

examples *The table* is big.   *The University of Ohio* is a large university.
It is big.   *It* is a large university.

2. WE: WE refers to the speaker and another person, or to the speaker and other people.
3. YOU: The pronoun YOU is singular or plural.
4. THEY: Use the pronoun THEY to talk about people or things.

CONTRACTIONS WITH *BE*

She's 32 years old.
He's a graduate student.
I'm Chrissy's mother.
They're students.
Bill isn't a student.
We aren't graduate students.
It isn't here.

Notes

A. Positive contractions
   1. The subject pronoun and the verb BE are frequently contracted in spoken and in informal written English.
   2. To form the contraction, drop the first vowel of the verb BE (AM, IS, ARE) and replace it with an apostrophe.

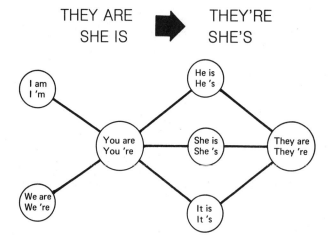

B. Negative contractions: There are two forms of negative contractions with the verb BE.
   1. NOT follows the contraction.
      a. This form is sometimes used for emphasis.

      examples   He's *not* a student.
                     They're *not* from California.

   2. NOT contracts with BE.
      a. This form is more frequently used than form (a) above.

      examples   Bill *isn't* a student.
                     They *aren't* from Texas.

      b. AM never contracts with NOT

      examples $\begin{Bmatrix} \text{I am} \\ \text{I'm} \end{Bmatrix}$ a student. $\begin{Bmatrix} \text{I am not} \\ \text{I'm not} \end{Bmatrix}$ a teacher.

      c. To form the contraction, drop the O in NOT and replace it with an apostrophe.

IS NOT   ➡   ISN'T
ARE NOT   AREN'T

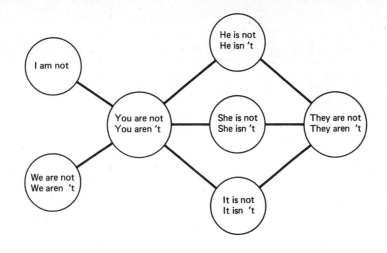

examples $\begin{Bmatrix} \text{He is} \\ \text{He's} \end{Bmatrix}$ a third grade teacher. $\begin{Bmatrix} \text{He is not} \\ \text{He's not} \\ \text{He isn't} \end{Bmatrix}$ a student.

$\begin{Bmatrix} \text{They are} \\ \text{They're} \end{Bmatrix}$ students. $\begin{Bmatrix} \text{They are not} \\ \text{They're not} \\ \text{They aren't} \end{Bmatrix}$ third grade teachers.

ARTICLE USAGE: AN INTRODUCTION

Darlene is a university student.
Gary is an elementary school teacher.
The campus is large.
This is the chemistry building.

Notes

A. Articles: A, AN, and THE (See Chapter Seven for more information.)
  1. Use the indefinite article A/AN before a singular noun when the noun is introduced or identified for the first time.

     examples Darlene is *a* student. (The speaker is introducing this knowledge about Darlene.)
     It's *an* office building. (The speaker is identifying the object.)

  2. Use the definite article THE before a noun when both the listener and the speaker know something about the noun.

     examples *The* campus is large. (The speaker and listener both know about the campus.)
     The teacher is very nice. (The speaker and listener both know the teacher.)

B. A/AN
  1. Use A before a word beginning with a consonant sound.

     examples Gary is *a* teacher.
     New York is *a* large city.

  a. Use A before a vowel when the vowel has a consonant sound.

     examples Darlene is *a* university student.
     　　　　　　　　　/yew/
     Gary is *a* union member.
     　　　　　　/yew/

  2. Use AN before a word beginning with a vowel sound.

     examples Gary is *an* elementary school teacher.
     I'm *an* undergraduate student.

a. The letter H at the beginning of a word is sometimes pronounced and sometimes silent. Compare:

a house   (HOUSE begins with a consonant sound.)
an hour   (HOUR begins with a vowel sound.)

3. Do not use A/AN before plural nouns or mass nouns.

examples   Darlene and Meg are *students.*
Smog is unhealthy.

C. THE sometimes comes before singular and plural count nouns.

examples   *The* chemistry building is old.
The students are on campus.
The traffic is heavy.

BASIC WRITING RULES. PART I.

Meg Bernstein is from Chicago, Illinois.   Chrissy's last name is Peterson.
She's a graduate student at the university.   Jonathan's apartment is on Princeton Avenue.

Notes

A. Capital letters
1. Capitalize all proper nouns.

examples   *Meg Bernstein* is from *Chicago, Illinois.*
Gary is a teacher at *Franklin Elementary School.*

2. Capitalize the first word in a sentence.

examples   *She's* in the second grade.
He's 37 years old.
It's an old building.

3. Always capitalize the subject pronoun I.

examples   *I'm* a graduate student.
Meg and *I* are friends.

B. Periods
1. Always end a statement with a period.

examples   Bill's a tennis teacher.
Jonathan is from Boston, Massachusetts.

2. Use a period after an abbreviation. When an abbreviation is at the end of a sentence, use only one period.

examples   Mr. & Mrs. Peterson are in Pennsylvania.
Gary's apartment is on Princeton Ave.

EXERCISE #1. NOUNS LEVEL A.

Directions Read the following sentences. Fill in the blanks with the singular or plural noun. Capitalize proper nouns.

example Chrissy is a _student_ in the
2nd _grade_ at Franklin
Elementary _School_.
She is 7 _years_ old.

1. Darlene is Chrissy's _____. She is
from _____. She is a
_____ at the university.

2. Gary is a _____ at Franklin
Elementary _____. He's 37
_____ old. He's from
_____.

3. Gary and Jonathan are _____.
_____ is from Massachusetts.
_____ is from Oregon. Jonathan is
a graduate _____. Gary isn't a
_____. He's a 3rd grade
_____.

4. Darlene and _____ are
friends. They are _____ at the
university. Darlene is from Harrisburg,
_____, and Meg is from Chicago,
_____. Harrisburg and Chicago
are _____. Pennsylvania and Illinois are _____.

Name: _____ Date: _____

5.

New York, Chicago, and

_____ are large

_____ in the United

_____. Los Angeles is a

_____ in California. Chicago is a city

in _____, and New York is a city

in _____.

EXERCISE #2. THE VERB *BE*. LEVEL A.

Directions Fill in the blanks with the correct form of the verb BE.

examples Jonathan _____*is*_____ from Massachusetts.

He and Meg _____*are*_____ students at the university.

1.

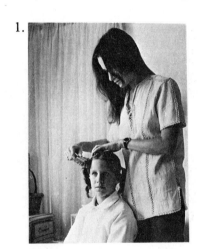

Chrissy and Darlene _____ in Los
(a)

Angeles. Darlene _____ Chrissy's mother.
(b)

Chrissy _____ 7 years old. She and Darlene
(c)

_____ students. Darlene
(d)

_____ a student at the university. Chrissy
(e)

_____ in the 2nd grade.
(f)

2.

I _____ a 3rd grade teacher. I
(a)

_____ not a student. Jonathan and I
(b)

_____ not from California. Jonathan
(c)

_____ from Massachusetts, and I
(d)

_____ from Oregon. We _____
(e)   (f)

friends.

3.  About 30,000 students _____ at the
                                                                    (a)
university. The university _____ very
                                                    (b)
large. It _____ an old university. Some
                      (c)
buildings _____ old. They _____
                    (d)   (e)
brick. Some buildings _____ new and
                                          (f)
modern.

EXERCISE #3. SUBJECT PRONOUNS. LEVEL A.

Directions Rewrite the sentences. Use a subject pronoun in place of the underlined words. Use capital
letters and periods when necessary.

example <u>Chrissy</u> is from Pennsylvania.

She is from Pennsylvania.

1. <u>Darlene</u> is from Pennsylvania.

_____

2. <u>Meg</u> is 26 years old.

_____

3. <u>Gary</u> is not a tennis teacher.

_____

4. <u>Darlene and Jonathan</u> are not from California.

_____

5. <u>Bill and I</u> are not students.

_____

6. <u>You and Darlene</u> are students.

_____

7. <u>The tennis teacher</u> is from San Diego.

_____

8. <u>The graduate student</u> is 31 years old.

_____

9. <u>San Diego</u> is a city in California.

_____

10. <u>The old buildings</u> are brick.

_____

Name: _____ Date: _____

EXERCISE #4. POSITIVE AND NEGATIVE CONTRACTIONS WITH THE VERB *BE*. LEVEL A.

Directions Rewrite the following sentences. Use the contracted form of BE. Use capital letters and periods.

examples 1. She is from California.
She's from California.
2. She is not from Oregon.
She isn't from Oregon.

1. He is a tennis teacher.

_____

2. We are university students.

_____

3. I am not a teacher.

_____

4. They are in Los Angeles.

_____

5. You are not 7 years old.

_____

6. It is not a small university.

_____

7. She is in the first grade.

_____

8. Chicago is not in California.

_____

EXERCISE #5. ARTICLES. LEVEL A.

Directions Fill in the blanks with A or AN.

example *Darlene:* This is ___*an*___ old building.
Bev: Yes, it's ___*a*___ very old university.

14

Darlene: Excuse me. Are you _____ student here?
                  (1)

Bev: Yes, I am. I'm _____ undergraduate in the Psychology Department. Are you _____ new student
on campus?   (2)   (3)

Darlene: Yes, I'm _____ graduate student in History.
                   (4)

Bev: History is _____ good department here.
                (5)

Darlene: It is _____ really nice campus. Is there _____ housing office on campus?
                 (6)   (7)

Bev: Yes, it's in Dodd Hall. It's _____ office for students only.
                           (8)

Darlene: Is it near here?

Bev: Yes, it's just over there. It's _____ old brick building. It's next to _____ tall, modern building.
                                (9)   (10)

Darlene: Thanks for the help.

EXERCISE #6. REVIEW OF CHAPTER ONE GRAMMAR. LEVEL A.

Directions Fill in the blanks.

    example This ___*is*___ Bill. ___*He*___ is ___*from*___ San Diego.
                          (1)   (2)   (3)

1.

        This is _____ . _____ is 7.
                       (1)   (2)

        She is _____ Pennsylvania. Darlene
                    (3)

        _____ Chrissy's mother.
           (4)

2.

        _____ is _____ .
           (1)   (2)

        He _____ 37. _____ is
            (3)   (4)

        _____ Oregon. _____ is
          (5)   (6)

        _____ 3rd grade teacher.
         (7)

Name: _____   Date: _____

3.

This _____ Meg. _____ is
        (1)   (2)

a _____ . _____ _____
   (3)   (4)   (5)

from Chicago. She _____ 26.
                     (6)

EXERCISE #7. NEGATIVE SENTENCES WITH THE VERB *BE*. LEVEL B.

Directions The information given is not correct.
          a. Write a sentence with the negative form of BE.
          b. Write a sentence with the correct information. Use a subject pronoun.

     example   Chrissy is 28 years old.
        a. *Chrissy is not 28 years old.*
        b. *She is 7 years old.*

1. The University of California is in Pennsylvania.

    a. _____

    b. _____
2. Bill is a graduate student.

    a. _____

    b. _____
3. Jonathan and Meg are tennis teachers.

    a. _____

    b. _____
4. San Diego is in Massachusetts.

    a. _____

    b. _____
5. I am 7 years old.

    a. _____

    b. _____
6. Meg is a teacher.

    a. _____

    b. _____
7. Gary is 23 years old.

    a. _____

    b. _____

8. Chrissy and Darlene are from New York.

    a. _____

    b. _____

9. We are in French class.

    a. _____

    b. _____

10. New York and Chicago are small cities.

    a. _____

    b. _____

EXERCISE #8.   ARTICLES.   LEVEL B.

Directions   Write a complete sentence using the information below. Use A or AN when necessary.

> **example**   It/ is/ very large university.
>
> *It is a very large university*

1. Gary/ is/ teacher/ at/ Franklin Elementary School.

   _____

2. Bev/ is/ undergraduate student/ in/ Psychology.

   _____

3. Bill/ is/ tennis teacher/ in/ Los Angeles.

   _____

4. Darlene and Meg/ are/ friends/ from/ Pennsylvania.

   _____

5. The Housing Office/ is/ in/ old brick building.

   _____

6. This/ is/ beautiful campus.

   _____

7. Chrissy/ is/ seven/ years old.

   _____

8. Chicago/ and/ New York/ are/ large cities/ in/ the United States.

   _____

EXERCISE #9.   PART I.   LEVEL C.

Directions   Describe these people. Write three sentences for each picture.

> **example**   Meg / Chicago / student
>
> a. *This is Meg.*
> b. *Meg is from Chicago.*
> c. *She's a student.*

Name: _____   Date: _____

1.

Bill / tennis teacher / 28

a. _____

_____

b. _____

_____

c. _____

_____

2.

Darlene / 32 / Pennsylvania

a. _____

_____

b. _____

_____

c. _____

_____

3.

Jonathan / Massachusetts / graduate student

a. _____

_____

b. _____

_____

c. _____

_____

EXERCISE #9. PART II. LEVEL C.

Directions Draw a picture of you and a picture of a classmate in the boxes below.
        1. Describe yourself.
        2. Describe your classmate.
      Write three sentences for each description.

1.

     You

a. _____

   _____

b. _____

   _____

c. _____

   _____

2.

  Your Classmate

a. _____

   _____

b. _____

   _____

c. _____

   _____

GETTING ACQUAINTED

At the Housing Office: Darlene and Chrissy are at the Housing Office. Darlene is in line.

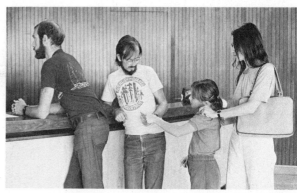

Chrissy: Hi. My name is Chrissy. What's your name?
Jonathan: Jonathan.
Chrissy: What do you do?
Jonathan: I'm a student here.
Chrissy: What's that?
Jonathan: It's my reg. card.

Chrissy: Jonathan, this is my mommy. Her name is Darlene. She's a student. This is Jonathan. He's a student, too.
Jonathan: Nice to meet you, Darlene.
Darlene: Glad to meet you.

Chrissy: Who are you?
Darlene: Chrissy, that's not polite.
Chrissy: Excuse me. What's your name?
Jonathan: This is my friend. His name is Gary.
Chrissy: Hi, Gary. Are you a student?
Gary: No, I'm a teacher.
Chrissy: Are you roommates?
Gary: Yes, we are.

ADJECTIVES WITH THE VERB *BE*

Apartments in Westwood are expensive.
There are new notices on the board.
I'm fine.
Are there good schools near the apartment?

Notes

A. Adjectives give the qualities or characteristics of nouns or pronouns.

examples   It's an *old   university.*
                    (adj.) (noun)
               The *campus* is *large.*
                    (noun)   (adjective)

1. The adjective form in English does not change to agree with the noun.

   examples   Gary is *thin.*
                  Darlene and Chrissy are *thin* also.

B. The verb BE can be followed by an adjective alone or by a noun modified by an adjective.

examples   He is *tall.*
                    (adj.)
               I'm *fine.*
                    (adj.)
               He is a *tall   man*
                        (adj.) (noun)
               That's the *new   cafeteria.*
                           (adj.) (noun)

SUBJECT	BE	ADJECTIVE
He	is	tall.
She	is	skinny.
She	is	middle-aged.
I	am	poor.
We	are	foreign.
They	are	quiet.
You	are	serious.

SUBJECT	BE	ARTICLE	ADJECTIVE	NOUN
He	is	a	tall	man.
She	is	a	skinny	girl.
She	is	a	middle-aged	woman.
I	am	a	poor	student.
We	are		foreign	students.
They	are		quiet	neighbors.
You	are		serious	students.

C. In noun phrases more than one adjective can modify a noun.

examples   Chrissy is a *talkative, friendly* girl.
               Bunche Hall is a *tall, modern* building.

D. After the verb BE connect adjectives with AND.

examples   Jonathan is *quiet and studious.*
               The street is *crowded and noisy.*

1. Separate more than two adjectives with commas. AND comes before the last adjective.

   examples   The apartment is *small, dark, and crowded.*
                  Jonathan's chemistry professor is *short, fat, and bald.*

POSSESSIVE ADJECTIVES AND POSSESSIVE NOUNS.   PART I.

Jonathan is Gary's roommate.
Chrissy's school is in Los Angeles.
His roommate is from Massachusetts.
My teacher is from Oregon.

POSSESSIVE NOUN	POSSESSIVE ADJECTIVE
(speaker's book)	*my* book(s)
(listener's roommate)	*your* roommate(s)
Bill's friend(s) the teacher's student(s) Jonathan's sister	*his* friend(s) *his* student(s) *his* sister
Darlene's roommate(s) the student's notebook(s) Darlene's sister	*her* roommate(s) *her* notebook(s) *her* sister

Notes

A. Use: Use possessive forms to show ownership, possession, or close relationships.

examples   Darlene is *Chrissy's* mother.
Her purse is on the desk.

B. Form
1. Noun form: Add 'S to show possession.

examples   The *secretary's* name is Ms. Olson.
Gary's sister is married.

  a. If the noun ends with -S, add only an apostrophe (').

examples   *James'* family is from Michigan.
Professor *Jones'* class is difficult.

2. Adjective form

examples   *His* apartment is small.
My classes are easy.

C. Sometimes a phrase with OF shows possession.

examples   *The name of the secretary* is Ms. Olson.
The color of the carpet is blue.

1. Use 'S or an apostrophe by itself to show possession with people's names. Do not use a phrase with OF.

DEMONSTRATIVE PRONOUNS: *THIS/THAT*

This is the Housing Office.
What's that? It's the new chemistry building.
Who's that? That's my roommate, Jonathan Moscowitz.
. . . and what's this? It's my registration card.

Notes

A. Use: We sometimes use the demonstratives THIS and THAT to point to objects and people.
  1. THIS
    a. Use THIS for objects and people near the speaker.

      examples   This is the cafeteria.
                      This is my house.

    b. Use THIS for introducing people.

      examples   This is my daughter, Chrissy.
                      This is my roommate, Gary.

  2. THAT
    a. Use THAT for objects and people far from the speaker.

      examples   That's the psychology building.
                      That's the new secretary.

    b. We sometimes use THAT to give an opinion.

      examples   That's not polite.
                      That's stupid.
                      That's a great idea.

B. Contracted form
  1. THIS never contracts with the verb BE in written English.
    a. In spoken English, THIS IS often sounds like /ðɪsəz/.

      examples   This is the basement.
                      This is my office.

  2. THAT can contract with the verb BE.

$$\text{THAT} + \text{IS} \implies \text{THAT'S}$$

      examples   That's the history professor.
                      That's the new dormitory.

WHO/WHAT + BE

Who are you?
    I'm Jonathan's roommate.
Who is that?
    . . . my friend Gary.
What's that?
    It's my reg. card.
What's your name?
    Jonathan Moscowitz.

Notes

A. Use: The interrogatives WHO and WHAT ask for information.
  1. WHO asks about a person.
  2. WHAT asks about an object.
  3. Use IT'S or THAT'S to answer a question with THIS or THAT.

    examples What's *that* on the counter?
                It's a list of apartments for rent.
             Who's *that?*
                That's the secretary.
             What's *this?*
                It's my student identification card.
             What's *this?*
                That's Meg's lipstick.

B. Question form
  1. In information questions, WHO or WHAT occurs at the beginning of the sentence.

    examples *What's* your name?
                Who are you?

  2. WHO and WHAT can be followed by the verb BE.
    a. The subject of the sentence follows the verb BE.

      examples What *is*   *your name?*
                    BE   (subject)
               Who *are* *you?*
                    BE   (subject)

    b. Both WHO and WHAT contract with IS.

$$WHO + IS \longrightarrow WHO'S$$

$$WHAT + IS \longrightarrow WHAT'S$$

      examples What's your name?
                   Who's your roommate?

    c. WHO and WHAT don't contract with other forms of BE in written English.

      examples *Who are* you?
                   What are they?

C. Idiomatic expressions with WHO and WHAT.
  1. Use the question WHO IS IT? to ask who is at the door or on the phone.

    examples Who is it?
                    It's your friend, Adrienne.
             Who is it?
                    It's the mailman.

2. Use the questions WHAT'S WRONG? and WHAT'S THE MATTER? to ask about a problem.

   examples   What's wrong?
   　　　　　　　　I have a flat tire.
   　　　　　　　What's the matter?
   　　　　　　　　I'm depressed.

OCCUPATIONS

Jonathan: What do you do?
Darlene: I'm a student.
Jonathan: That's my friend, Gary.
Darlene: What does he do?
Jonathan: He's a 3rd grade teacher.

Notes

A. The question WHAT DO YOU DO? or WHAT DOES $\begin{Bmatrix} \text{HE} \\ \text{SHE} \end{Bmatrix}$ DO? asks about someone's occupation or job.

   examples   What do you do?
   　　　　　　　　I'm a chemistry professor.
   　　　　　　　What does she do?
   　　　　　　　　She's a writer.
   　　　　　　　What does he do?
   　　　　　　　　He's a hairstylist.

B. Use A or AN with a profession if you are talking about one person.

   examples   I'm *a* teacher.
   　　　　　　　He's *an* actor.
   　　　　　　　She's *a* nurse.

C. Some occupation names have different male and female forms.

Male Form	Female Form
actor	actress
waiter	waitress

Occupations

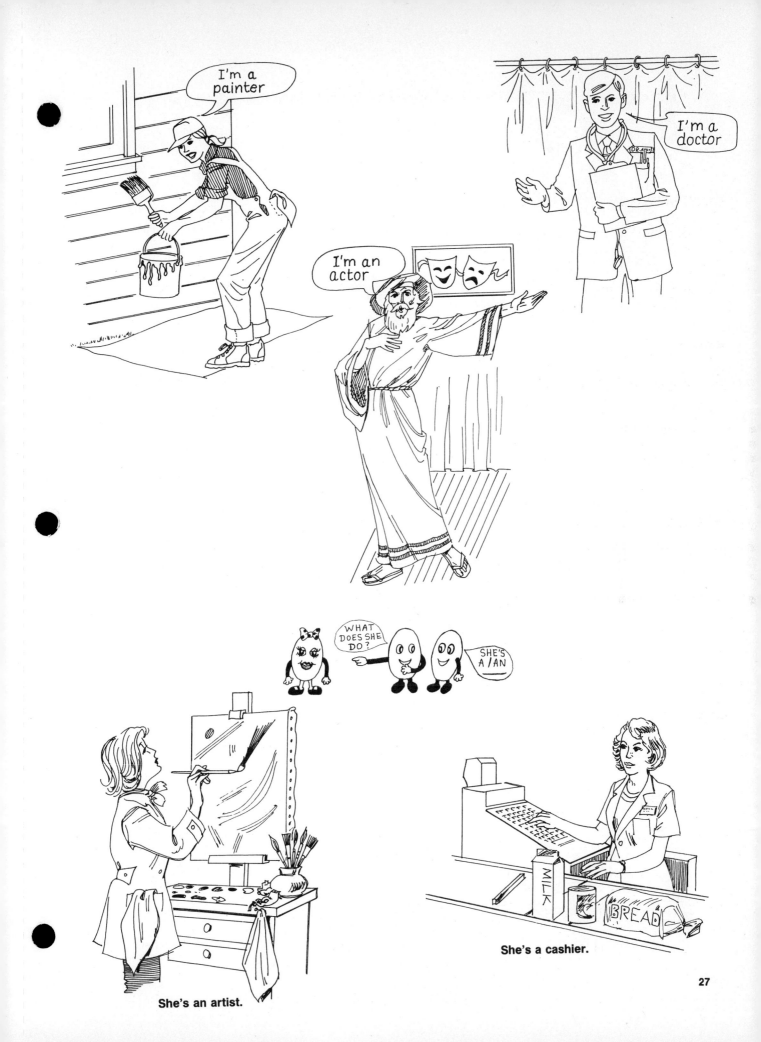

She's a judge.

She's a flight attendant.

She's a police officer.

She's a beautician.

WHAT DOES HE DO?

HE'S A / AN ___

He's a taxi driver.

He's a preacher.

He's a carpenter.

He's a student.

He's a waiter.

He's a cook.

TOO/ALSO

Darlene: Jonathan, this is my friend Meg. She's a student in the School of Management. Meg, this is Jonathan. He's a student too. He's a graduate student in physics.

Meg: Are you a new student also?

Jonathan: No.

Notes

A. TOO and ALSO can emphasize an identical or similar situation.

examples Are you a new student $\begin{Bmatrix} \text{too?} \\ \text{also?} \end{Bmatrix}$ She's from Pennsylvania $\begin{Bmatrix} \text{too} \\ \text{also} \end{Bmatrix}$.

1. The adverb TOO usually comes at the end of the sentence.

examples Gary is a teacher.   Jonathan is a graduate student.
Bill is a teacher *too.*   Meg is a graduate student *too.*

2. The adverb ALSO sometimes comes after the verb BE, and sometimes at the end of the sentence.

    examples   Darlene and Chrissy are on campus.   Meg's apartment is near the beach.
                     Jonathan and Gary are *also* on campus.   Bill's apartment is near the beach *also*.

BASIC WRITING RULES. PART II.

Registration Card	Do not photocopy
OFFICIAL SEAL UNIVERSITY	MS. / MISS / MR. / MRS. *Bernstein, Margaret*
	(last) NAME (first)
valid fall semester only	*1342 Beach Avenue Apt C.*
	(number) ADDRESS (street)
student ID no. 60137803	*Los Angeles CA 90291*
	CITY STATE ZIP

Notes

A. Periods
   1. Remember to end a statement with a period. (See Chapter One, "Writing Rules.")
   2. Use periods after most abbreviations.
      a. The following titles are abbreviated with people's names.

TITLE	EXAMPLE	USE
MS.*	Ms. Peterson Ms. Margaret Bernstein	MS. is used before a woman's last name or before her first and last name. It can refer to a married or single woman.
MRS.	Mrs. Chapman Mrs. Robert Starsky	MRS. is used before the last name of a married woman, or before her husband's first and last name.
MR.	Mr. Garvey Mr. Jonathan Moscowitz	MR. is used before a man's last name, or before his first and last name.
DR.	Dr. Hamilton Dr. Samuel Bernstein	DR. is used before the last, or first and last name of a medical doctor or someone with a Ph.D. degree.
SR. / JR.	Jonathan Moscowitz, Sr. (father) Jonathan Moscowitz, Jr. (son)	SR. and JR. are used after a man's name to distinguish between a father and son with the same first and last name.

* MISS is used before the last name of a single woman, or before her first and
last name. MISS is not abbreviated.

B. The following words are sometimes abbreviated in addresses:

COMMON ABBREVIATIONS USED IN ADDRESSES			
Avenue	Ave.	Parkway	Pkwy.
Boulevard	Blvd.	Highway	Hwy.
Street	St.	Point	Pt.
Place	Pl.	Canyon	Cyn.
Way	Wy.	Mount	Mt.
Lane	Ln.	Mountain	Mtn.
Road	Rd.	Junction	Jct.
Drive	Dr.	Apartment	Apt.
Circle	Cir.	Number	No.
Court	Ct.	North	N.
Terrace	Ter.	South	S.
Ridge	Rdg.	East	E.
Heights	Hts.	West	W.

example

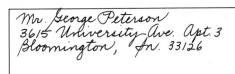

1. The names of states are abbreviated according to U.S. Post Office rules. The Post Office omits the period after state abbreviations. Some of the names of cities and countries can also be abbreviated.

Wisconsin	WIS
New York	NY
Maryland	MD
Los Angeles	L.A.
Sacramento	Sac.
Philadelphia	Phil.
Mexico	Mex.
United Kingdom	U.K.
United States of America	U.S.A.

2. The names of the days of the week and months are sometimes abbreviated.

DAYS OF THE WEEK	
FULL FORM	**ABBREVIATED FORM**
Monday	Mon.
Tuesday	Tues.
Wednesday	Wed.
Thursday	Thurs.
Friday	Fri.
Saturday	Sat.
Sunday	Sun.

MONTHS	
FULL FORM	**ABBREVIATED FORM**
January	Jan.
February	Feb.
March	Mar.
April	Apr.
May	—
June	—
July	—
August	Aug.
September	Sept.
October	Oct.
November	Nov.
December	Dec.

EXERCISE #1. ADJECTIVES. LEVEL A.

Directions Combine the two sentences into one sentence.

> **example** My neighbor is a woman.
> My neighbor is middle-aged.
>
> *My neighbor is a middle-aged woman.*

1. Darlene is patient. Darlene is a mother.

_____

2. Chrissy is a child. Chrissy is talkative.

_____

3. He is a man. He is aggressive.

_____

4. They are neighbors. They are unfriendly.

_____

5. We are serious. We are students.

_____

6. I am a student. I am foreign.

_____

7. They are buildings. They are brick.

_____

8. He's an athlete. He's professional.

_____

EXERCISE # 2. POSSESSIVES. LEVEL A.

Directions Fill in the blanks with the correct possessive form and the name of the person. Use the following information:

NAME	OCCUPATION	ORIGIN	SEX	AGE
Marilyn	cashier	Peoria, Illinois	female	19
Christine	photographer	Seattle, Washington	female	22
Sylvia	waitress	New York, New York	female	19
Philippe	nurse	Toronto, Canada	male	31
Brad	businessman	Kansas City, Missouri	male	22
Esther	sales clerk	New York, New York	female	24
Louis	student	Nice, France	male	24
Tony	teacher	Los Angeles, Calif.	male	31
Günther	secretary	Hamburg, Germany	male	27
Randy	student	Kansas City, Missouri	male	25
Jane	secretary	Peoria, Illinois	female	22
Greg	waiter	Los Angeles, Calif.	male	31
Dustin	actor	Portland, Oregon	male	25

> **example** I am from New York. I am a waitress. _My_ name is _Sylvia_ .

1. I am from Peoria. I am a cashier. _____ name is _____ .

Name: _____   Date: _____   33

2. He is from Los Angeles. He is a teacher. _____ name is _____.

3. She is from New York. She is a sales clerk. _____ name is _____.

4. He is an actor. He is from Portland. _____ name is _____.

5. You are 22. You are female. You are a photographer. _____ name is _____.

6. I am a secretary. I am female. _____ name is _____.

7. I am 31. I am from Los Angeles. I am a waiter. _____ name is _____.

8. He is from Kansas City. He is a student. _____ name is _____.

9. She is from New York. She is 19 years old. _____ name is _____.

10. You are a male. You are 31. You are from Toronto. _____ name is _____.

EXERCISE #3. *THIS/THAT.* LEVEL A.

Directions Look at the pictures. Fill in the blanks with THIS or THAT.

  example *Darlene:* ___*This*___ is my daughter, Chrissy.

Darlene: The gas tank is almost empty. Is

_____ a gas station ahead?
　　　　(1)

Chrissy: Yeah, it is.

Darlene: _____'s great.
　　　　　(2)

Chrissy: Mommy, _____ is the wrong
　　　　　　　　(3)

pump. It's supreme . . . not regular.

Darlene: Oh, _____'s right.
　　　　　　(4)

Here's the regular gas.

Chrissy: But Mommy, _____ is full
　　　　　　　　　(5)

service. It's really expensive.

_____'s the self-service
　　(6)

island.

Darlene: Okay. Let's move the car.

Chrissy: What's _____?
                     (7)

Attendant: _____'s the air hose.
               (8)

Chrissy: Who's _____?
                (9)

Attendant: Where?

Chrissy: Behind you.

Attendant: _____'s another attendant.
             (10)

Darlene: Chrissy, don't point. _____'s
                                      (11)

not polite.

Attendant: _____'s okay.
             (12)

Name: _____   Date: _____

EXERCISE #4. *WHO/WHAT.* LEVEL A.

Directions Read the dialogue between Jonathan and Gary. Fill in the blanks with WHO or WHAT.

example   *Gary:*   _____*What*_____'s that?
              Jonathan: It's my chemistry notebook.

Jonathan and Gary are at home

Gary: This desk is a mess.

Jonathan: It's *not* a mess. It's all important material.

Gary: Important?! _____'s this envelope?
                               (1)

Jonathan: It's from the bank. It's my bank statement.

Gary: And _____'s this?
                       (2)

Jonathan: A picture.

Gary: _____ is it?
                   (3)

Jonathan: My ex-girl friend.

Gary: _____'s her name.
                   (4)

Jonathan: Louise.

Gary: _____ does she do?
(5)

Jonathan: She's a cocktail waitress.

Gary: Hmmm . . . she's pretty.

Jonathan: Yeah, but stupid!

Gary: Pretty women usually are . . .

Jonathan: Stupid . . . ? That's a very sexist statement.

Gary: Well, they are . . . except Adrienne.

Jonathan: _____'s Adrienne?
(6)

Gary: She's my girlfriend. She's beautiful and brilliant.

Jonathan: _____ does she do?
(7)

Gary: She's a secretary.

Jonathan: Secretary?! Secretaries aren't brilliant.

Gary: Now *that's* sexist . . . and it's not true!

Jonathan: Hmmm . . .

Gary: Hey, _____'s that noise?
(8)

Jonathan: It's the doorbell.

Gary: No, it isn't. It's the telephone

Jonathan: Hello? _____ is this, please? Just a minute.
(9)

Gary: _____ is it?
(10)

Jonathan: It's your brilliant girlfriend, Adrienne.

EXERCISE #5. WRITING RULES. PART I. LEVEL A.

Directions   Fill out the registration cards with the information. Use abbreviated forms, periods, and capital letters when necessary.

> **example**   MS. MARGARET BERNSTEIN / 1342 BEACH AVENUE / APARTMENT C / LOS ANGELES / CALIFORNIA / 90291

Registration Card   Do not photocopy

MS.
MISS
MR.
MRS. *Bernstein   Margaret*
        (last)   NAME   (first)
1342 Beach Ave.   Apt. C
        (number)   ADDRESS   (street)
Los Angeles, CA   90291
        CITY   STATE   ZIP

valid fall semester only

student ID no. 60137803

Name: _____   Date: _____

1. MRS. PENNY STARSKY / 481 OAK AVENUE / APARTMENT 2B / ITHACA / NEW YORK / 14850

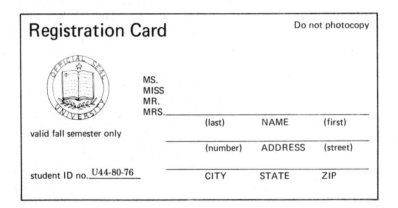

2. MISS LINDA MOSCOWITZ / MADISON / WISCONSIN / 2109 1/2 LAKESIDE DRIVE / 53706

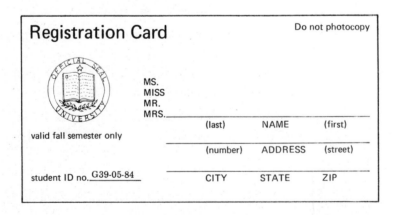

3. MR. GEORGE PETERSON / BALTIMORE / MARYLAND / 8374 NORTH LIBERTY PLACE / APARTMENT A / 21205

EXERCISE #5.   WRITING RULES.   PART II.   LEVEL A.

Directions   Fill out the two registration cards below. Use information about you and about a classmate.

4. You:

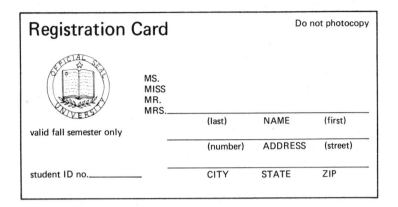

Registration Card   Do not photocopy

MS.
MISS
MR.
MRS.
                    (last)   NAME   (first)

valid fall semester only
                    (number)   ADDRESS   (street)

student ID no._____
                    CITY   STATE   ZIP

5. Your classmate:

Registration Card   Do not photocopy

MS.
MISS
MR.
MRS.
                    (last)   NAME   (first)

valid fall semester only
                    (number)   ADDRESS   (street)

student ID no._____
                    CITY   STATE   ZIP

EXERCISE #6.   REVIEW.   LEVEL A.

Directions   Fill in the blanks.

examples   Secretary:___*What*__'s __*your*___name?
                 Gary: ___*My*___name ___*is*___Gary.

I. Introducing yourself

Chrissy: Hi. _____ name _____ Chrissy. What's _____ name?
                  (1)   (2)   (3)

Ms. Olson: _____ name _____ Ms. Olson.
                  (4)   (5)

Chrissy: Are you _____ student?
                          (6)

Ms. Olson: No, I_____ a secretary. Is this _____ mommy?
                      (7)   (8)

Chrissy: Yes, it is. _____ name _____ Darlene.
                              (9)   (10)

Ms. Olson: Hi, Darlene. Nice to meet you.
Darlene: Glad to meet you.

II. Introducing another person

Jonathan: Darlene, this _____ my roommate, Gary. He _____ _____ 3rd grade
                                (1)   (2)   (3)

teacher.

Darlene: I _____ glad to meet you.
                   (4)

Gary: Nice to meet you. Are you new in Los Angeles?

Darlene: Yes, _____ am.
                       (5)

Gary: Where _____ you _____?
                        (6)   (7)

Darlene: _____ _____ _____ Pennsylvania.
                  (8)   (9)   (10)

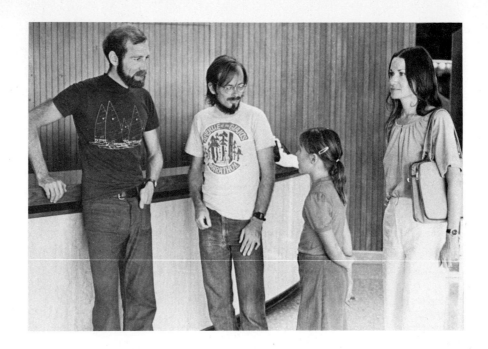

III. Introducing several people

Jonathan: Hi, Chrissy.

Chrissy: Hi.

Jonathan: _____ is _____ friend, Gary.
              (1)   (2)

Gary: Hi, Chrissy.

Chrissy: Hi. How old are you?

Jonathan: Chrissy, _____'s not polite.
                  (3)

Gary: That's okay. I _____ 37 _____ _____. How old _____ you?
                (4)   (5)   (6)   (7)

Chrissy: _____'m 7.
        (8)

Gary: _____'s that?
       (9)

Chrissy: That's _____ mommy.
            (10)

Gary: _____'s _____ name?
      (11)   (12)

Chrissy: Darlene.

EXERCISE #7. ADJECTIVES. LEVEL B.

Directions Write two sentences using the subject and adjective given. Follow the examples.

    examples 1. he / tall   a. *He is tall.*
                                   b. *He is a tall man.*
                2. they / poor a. *They are poor.*
                                     b. *They are poor students.*

Name: _____ Date: _____

1. Chrissy / skinny

    a. _____

    b. _____

2. Gary / serious

    a. _____

    b. _____

3. Darlene / quiet

    a. _____

    b. _____

4. I / intelligent

    a. _____

    b. _____

5. the neighbors / noisy

    a. _____

    b. _____

6. we / rich

    a. _____

    b. _____

7. they / middle-aged

    a. _____

    b. _____

8. he / French

    a. _____

    b. _____

EXERCISE #8. *WHO/WHAT.* LEVEL B.

Directions Look at the dialogues and write questions with WHO or WHAT.

    examples   *Marilyn:* *What's your name* ?
                        Sylvia: My name is Sylvia.
                                   What's your name ?
                        Marilyn: My name is Marilyn.
                        Sylvia: *What do you do* ?
                        Marilyn: I'm a cashier at Fine Food Supermarket.
                        Sylvia: *Who's that* ?
                        Marilyn: That's my friend Philippe. He's a nurse.

1. *Günther:*   My name is Günther.

   _____ ?
   (a)

   Dustin: My name is Dustin.

   Günther: _____ ?
   (b)

   Dustin: I'm an actor.

   _____ ?
   (c)

   Günther: I'm a secretary.

2. *Randy:*   Hi. Are you a student here?

   Louis: Yes, I am.

   Randy: _____ ?
   (a)

   Louis: Louis.

   _____ ?
   (b)

   Randy: My name is Randy.

   _____ ?
   (c)

   Louis: That's my roommate.

   Randy: _____ ?
   (d)

   Louis: Her name is Christine.

   Randy: _____ ?
   (e)

   Louis: She's a photographer.

EXERCISE #9.   WRITING RULES.   LEVEL B.

Directions   Fill out the forms with information about *you*. Use abbreviated forms. Use capital letters when necessary.

example

```
IDENTIFICATION

MY NAME IS  Meg Bernstein
ADDRESS  1342 Beach Avenue Apt. C
CITY  Los Angeles  STATE California
ZIP  90291      PHONE NO. (213) 829-1317
```

Name: _____   Date: _____

1.

IDENTIFICATION

MY NAME IS_____

ADDRESS_____

CITY_____STATE_____

ZIP_____PHONE NO._____

2.

UNIVERSITY LIBRARY CARD

NAME_____
      (last)   (first)   (middle initial)

ADDRESS_____
      (no.)   (street)

_____
     (city)   (state)   (zip)

PHONE_____
     (day)   (eve.)

3.

Employment Application Form

Date_____

Miss
Mrs._____
Mr.   Last   First   Middle

Local Address_____Permanent Address_____
     Number   Street   Number   Street

_____
     City   State   City   State/Country

Home Phone (___)_____Business Phone (___)_____

Age_____   Citizenship_____

Birthdate_____   Place of Birth_____

4.

APPLICATION FOR ENROLLMENT

Directions:

1) Complete each item below in English.
2) Print clearly.
3) Be sure to sign the application.
4) Return this form with the application fee of $25.

****

NAME:_____TELEPHONE:_____
    (family)   (first)   (middle)

CURRENT MAILING ADDRESS:_____
                  (number)   (street)

_____
       (city)   (state/country)

DATE OF BIRTH:_____COUNTRY OF BIRTH:_____
    (month) (day) (year)

COUNTRY OF CITIZENSHIP:_____Sex:_____

SIGNATURE:_____

5.

HEALTH CLINIC
Information Sheet

Please print all information clearly and legibly.

DATE _____

NAME _____
       last name   first name   middle initial

       maiden name

LOCAL
ADDRESS _____
       number   street   city   state   zip

PERMANENT
ADDRESS _____
       number   street   city   state   zip

TELEPHONE _____ TELEPHONE _____
       home   business

BIRTHDATE _____ AGE _____ SEX _____

MARITAL STATUS _____ HEIGHT _____ WEIGHT ____

IN CASE OF EMERGENCY NOTIFY _____
                         name

                         street

                city   state   zip

                phone

X _____
   signature

6.

DRIVER'S LICENSE APPLICATION FORM
Please Print Carefully

Print complete name: _____
         FIRST   MIDDLE   LAST

Mailing address: _____ Apt. No.: _____

City: _____ Zip Code: _____

         Color   Color
Sex: _____ hair: ____ eyes: ____ Height: _____ Weight: _____

Birthdate: _____ Age Today: _____
     MONTH   DAY   YEAR

EXERCISE #10. REVIEW. LEVEL B.

Directions Use the information from the chart on page 33 and write one sentence supplying the missing information.

example

Her name is Christine. She's 22 years old.
She's from Seattle, Washington. _She's a_
photographer.

1.

He's from Kansas City, Missouri. He's 25 years old. He's a student. _____
_____

2.

Her name is Sylvia. She's a waitress.
_____
_____. She's 19.

3.

His name is Günther. He's 27 years old.
_____
He's from Hamburg, Germany.

4.

He's from Nice, France. _____
_____
He's a student. His name is Louis.

46

5.

His name is Dustin. _____

_____

He's 25 years old. He's an actor.

6.

His name is Greg. He's 31 years old.

_____

He's from Los Angeles, California.

EXERCISE #11. LEVEL C.

Directions   Use the information from the chart on page 33 and write a paragraph about each person.

Model paragraph

Her name is Christine. She's from Seattle, Washington. She's a photographer. She's twenty-two years old.

Christine

1.

Philippe

_____

_____

_____

_____

2.

Brad

_____

_____

_____

_____

Name: _____   Date: _____

3.  **Marilyn**

_____

_____

_____

_____

4.  **Jane**

_____

_____

_____

_____

5.  **Esther**

_____

_____

_____

_____

6.  **Tony**

_____

_____

_____

_____

7. **Your classmate**

_____

_____

_____

_____

8.

You

          _____

          _____

          _____

          _____

          _____

EXERCISE #12. PART I. LEVEL C.

Directions 1. Read the model paragraph.

              2. Write a paragraph about Bill. Use the adjectives listed. Use NOT when the adjective does not describe Bill.

Model paragraph

ADJECTIVES	
young	dark
pretty	green
quiet	wavy
tall	studious
long	athletic

Darlene is a part-time student. She is a young woman from Pennsylvania. She is pretty and quiet. She is not tall. Her hair is long, dark, and wavy. Her eyes are green. She is studious and not athletic.

Name: _____   Date: _____

1.

ADJECTIVES	
young	blond
handsome	curly
energetic	green
tall	studious
short	athletic

_____

_____

_____

_____

_____

_____

_____

EXERCISE #12.   PART II.   LEVEL C.

Directions   Write a paragraph about yourself. Use the adjectives in the box below. Use NOT when the adjective does not describe you.

ADJECTIVES	
young	long
pretty/handsome	straight
quiet	dark
energetic	studious
tall	athletic

_____

_____

_____

_____

_____

_____

_____

_____

_____

_____

_____

_____

AT THE HOUSING OFFICE

Meg and Darlene are on the phone

Darlene: Hi, Meg? This is Darlene.

Meg: Oh hi, Darlene.

Darlene: How are you?

Meg: Just fine. How are you and Chrissy?

Darlene: We're fine. We're at the Housing Office on campus.

Meg: Oh, are there any new notices on the bulletin board?

Darlene: There are some apartments for rent in Westwood near campus. They're very expensive. There are also some in Santa Monica. Is that far from campus?

Meg: Not really. It's close to the beach. It's about five miles from school.

Darlene: Okay, good. That's not too far. Thanks, Meg.

Meg: You're welcome.

EXPLETIVE *THERE*

There is a housing office on campus. It is in Dodd Hall. It is in the basement.

There is a list on the bulletin board. The board is on the wall outside the office. The office is in room number 79.

Inside the office there is a counter. There are housing lists on the counter. There is a secretary in the room, and there is a typewriter on her desk. There is a pay phone in the corner.

Notes

A. Use THERE IS/THERE ARE to show the existence of something.

    examples   There's a housing office on campus.
                     There are lists on the counter.

B. THERE IS comes before singular nouns and mass nouns.
  1. With singular count nouns, use A/AN.

    examples   There is *a* pay phone in the corner.
                     There's *an* umbrella on the chair.

  2. With mass nouns, do not use A/AN.

    examples   There's *traffic* on the highway.
                     There's *smog* today.

  3. Other nouns in a series can come after the singular noun.

    examples   There's a typewriter, a stapler, and a lamp on the desk.
                     There's butter and milk in the refrigerator.

C. THERE ARE comes before plural nouns.
  1. With plural nouns, do not use A/AN.

    examples   There are *housing lists* on the counter.
                     There are *apartments* for rent in Santa Monica.

  2. Other nouns in a series can come after a plural noun.

    examples   There are some apartments for rent in Westwood.
                     There are desks, chairs, a counter and a pay phone in the Housing Office.

D. THERE can contract with IS.

THERE IS ➡ THERE'S

    examples   There's a table near the window.
                     There's an apartment for rent on Elm Street.

YES/NO-QUESTIONS AND SHORT ANSWERS WITH THE VERB *BE*

Darlene	is	my Mommy.
That	is	my reg. card.
I	am	at the Housing Office.
There	are	students at the counter.

Are	there	any cheap apartments?	No, there aren't.
Is	there	a long line?	Yes, there is.
Is	Jonathan	your roommate?	Yes, he is.
Are	the students	in line?	Yes, they are.
Are	we	at the Housing Office?	No, we aren't.

Isn't	there	a new notice on the board?	Yes, there is.
Isn't	that	her typewriter?	No, it isn't.
Aren't	you	roommates?	No, we aren't.
Isn't	she	your friend?	Yes, she is.
Aren't	we	in Dodd Hall?	No, we aren't.

My name	isn't	Margaret.
Chrissy	isn't	polite.
They	aren't	in line.
This	isn't	my reg. card.
I	'm	not her mother.
There	aren't	any cheap apartments.

Notes

A. Question form
   1. In YES/NO-questions BE comes before the subject.

   examples   *Are*   *you*   Gary's roommate?
                (BE) (subject)

                  Is   *Meg*   at home?
                (BE) (subject)

   2. In negative questions, use a contraction of BE plus NOT before the subject.

   examples   *Isn't*   *this*   a furnished apartment?
             (BE + NOT) (subject)

               Aren't   *you*   a graduate student in archaeology?
             (BE + NOT) (subject)

B. Response form
   1. Do not contract positive short answers.

   examples   Is Gary from Oregon?
                  Yes, he is.
                  Are Gary and Jonathan roommates?
                  Yes, they are.

   2. Negative short answers are sometimes contracted.

   examples   Is Jonathan a third grade teacher?

                 No, he $\begin{Bmatrix} \text{is not.} \\ \text{isn't.} \end{Bmatrix}$

                 Are Meg and Darlene teenagers?

                 No, they $\begin{Bmatrix} \text{are not.} \\ \text{aren't.} \end{Bmatrix}$

   3. You can give additional information after the YES or NO answer.

   examples   Are you a teacher?
                  Yes, I teach third grade at Franklin Elementary School.
                  Is Meg a full-time student?
                  No, she works part-time at the Graduate School of Management.

C. Use: A positive or negative question can ask for the same information. YES or NO answers both question forms.

   examples $\begin{Bmatrix} \text{Is} \\ \text{Isn't} \end{Bmatrix}$ Meg a student?
                      Yes, she is.

             $\begin{Bmatrix} \text{Are} \\ \text{Aren't} \end{Bmatrix}$ you roommates?
                      No, we aren't.

   1. Use a positive question when you do not know the answer.

   examples   Is this Dodd Hall?
                  No, it isn't.
                  Is there a pay telephone near here?
                  Yes, there's a phone in that room.

   2. Use a negative question when you think the answer is positive, but you aren't sure.

   examples   Aren't you Darlene Peterson?
                  Yes, I am.
                  Isn't this the chemistry building?
                  No, it's the history building.

PREPOSITIONS: *IN/ON/AT*

We're at the Housing Office.
Are there any new notices on the bulletin board?
Meg and Darlene are on the phone.
There are some apartments for rent in Westwood.
There are also some in Santa Monica.

Notes

A. Use IN to indicate inside something.

  examples The Housing Office is *in* Dodd Hall.
  The Housing Office is *in* the basement.
  The Housing Office is *in* room number 79.
  Chrissy and Darlene are *in* the office.

B. Use ON to indicate the surface of something or the top of something.

  examples The bulletin board is *on* the wall.
  The typewriters are *on* the desks.
  The information is *on* white cards.

C. Use AT for a specific location.

  examples They are *at* the Housing Office.
  Meg is a student *at* the university.
  Jonathan is *at* the counter.

D. There are many idiomatic expressions with IN, ON, and AT.

IN	ON	AT
in line	on the phone	at home
in ${front \atop back}$ of	on ${television \atop TV}$	at work
in bed	on the radio	at school
in class	on the coast	
	on (the) campus	

QUANTIFIERS. PART I. *SOME/SEVERAL/ANY/∅* (NO QUANTIFIER)

Are there any new notices on the bulletin board?
Aren't there any apartments near campus for rent?
There is some smog today.
Some buildings on campus are brick.
Apartments near campus are expensive.
There are several apartments for rent near the beach.

Notes

A. SOME, SEVERAL, ANY, or no quantifier (∅) indicate an indefinite amount of a noun.
   1. Positive statements with the quantifiers SOME and SEVERAL

a. You can use SOME before plural count nouns and mass nouns.

examples   There are some *students* in line.
(plural court noun)
There's some *smog* in the valley today.
(mass noun)

b. Use SEVERAL only before plural count nouns.

examples   There are several new *notices* on the board.
Several *apartments* in this building are for rent.

c. Sometimes there is no quantifier (∅) before plural count nouns and mass nouns.

examples   There are $\left\{\begin{array}{l}\varnothing\\ \text{some}\\ \text{several}\end{array}\right\}$ furnished apartments in this area.

There is $\left\{\begin{array}{l}\varnothing\\ \text{some}\end{array}\right\}$ traffic on the highway today.

2. Negative statements with ANY: Use ANY before plural count nouns and mass nouns.

examples   There aren't any *clouds* in the sky.
(plural count noun)
There isn't any *smog* in Tamaqua, Pennsylvania.
(mass noun)

3. Questions with SOME, ANY, and no quantifier (∅):

examples   Are there $\left\{\begin{array}{l}\varnothing\\ \text{some}\\ \text{any}\end{array}\right\}$ new notices on the board?

Isn't there $\left\{\begin{array}{l}\varnothing\\ \text{some}\\ \text{any}\end{array}\right\}$ milk in the refrigerator?

4. With answers, SOME, SEVERAL, and ANY are sometimes used alone without a noun.

examples   Is there money in your checking account?
No, there isn't any. (*Any* means *any money.*)
Are American cars economical?
Some are. (*Some* means *some American cars.*)
Are there any foreign students in Jonathan's physics lab?
Yes, there are several from Japan, and some from Taiwan too.
(*Several* and *some* mean *several foreign students* and *some foreign students.*)

BASIC WRITING RULES. PART III.

This is my daughter, Chrissy.   Chrissy was born December 24, 1973.
Are you a student?   Gary is Jonathan's roommate.
What's your name?

Notes

A. Commas
1. Use a comma to separate two nouns when they refer to the same object or person.

examples   This is the chemistry building, Morgan Hall.
This is my roommate, Gary.

2. Use a comma in dates to separate the day from the year.

examples   July 4, 1776
Dec. 10, 1945
Nov. 22, 1963

3. Use a comma between the last and first names of a person when the last name comes first.

NAME *Peterson, Darlene*

                            (last)   (first)

4. Use a comma to separate the names of cities, states, and countries.

    examples   Marilyn is from Peoria, Illinois.
                       Günther is from Hamburg, Germany.

5. Use a comma to separate nouns or adjectives in a series.

    examples   Meg is young, pretty, and vivacious.
                       Darlene is a mother, a student, and a secretary.

B. Question marks: Use a question mark at the end of a question.

    examples   Are you Jonathan's roommate?
                       What does Adrienne do?

C. Apostrophes

1. Use an apostrophe in a contraction to replace the missing letter or letters.

    examples   She's a brilliant woman.
                       It's my bank statement.

2. Use an apostrophe with possessive nouns.

    examples   Adrienne is Gary's girlfriend.
                       Christine is Ms. Peterson's daughter.

EXERCISE #1. *THERE IS/THERE ARE.* LEVEL A.

Directions   Fill in the blank with the correct form of BE.

example   There _____*is*_____ a research library on campus.

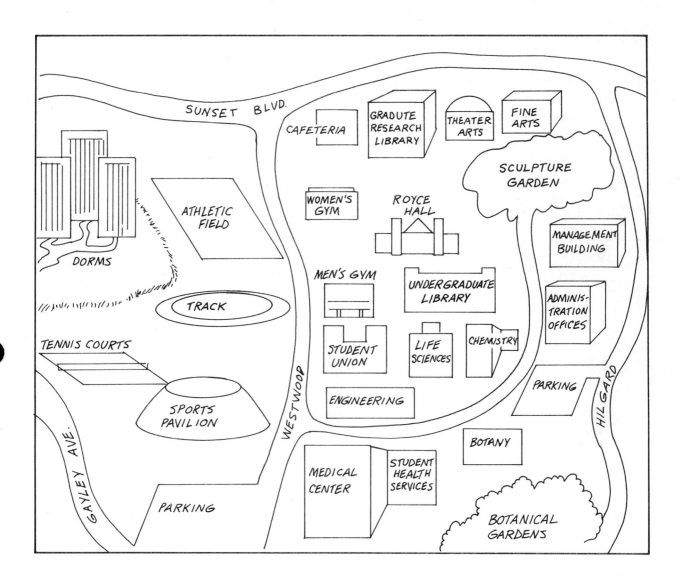

This is a large university campus. There _____ approximately 30,000 students at the univer-
                                           (1)

sity. There _____ four main streets on campus: Gayley, Westwood, Sunset, and Hilgard. On the
              (2)

hill near Sunset Blvd., there _____ dormitories and tennis courts. The track _____ world-
                               (3)   (4)

famous. Near the track there _____ a large athletic field. There _____ also a sports pavil-
                              (5)   (6)

ion. The classroom buildings are on the east side of campus. There _____ two gyms—a men's
                                                                     (7)

Name: _____   Date: _____   59

gym and a women's gym. There _____ also two gardens—a sculpture garden and a botanical
(8)

garden. There _____ science buildings in the south end of campus. In the science area there
(9)

_____ a medical center. There _____ also buildings for the departments of
(10) (11)

engineering, life sciences, chemistry, and botany. Most of the language and arts buildings are in the

north end of campus. There _____ a fine arts building and a theater arts department. There
(12)

_____ a management building near the administration building. A big problem at the university
(13)

is parking. There _____n't enough spaces for parking.
(14)

EXERCISE #2. QUESTIONS WITH *BE*. LEVEL A.

DRIVER'S LICENSE	DRIVER'S LICENSE
MUST BE CARRIED WHEN OPERATING A MOTOR VEHICLE AND WHEN APPLYING FOR RENEWAL	MUST BE CARRIED WHEN OPERATING A MOTOR VEHICLE AND WHEN APPLYING FOR RENEWAL

Left license:

EXPIRES ON BIRTHDAY IN **1986**

MD184297
Gary Chapman
1843 Rose Ave.
Los Angeles, CA 90291

PRE LIC EXP

SEX	HAIR	EYES	HEIGHT	WEIGHT	
M	BRN	BRN	6-02	162	80

DATE OF BIRTHDAY 07-11-44   MUST WEAR ☐ CORRECTIVE LENSES
OTHER ADDRESS   SEE OVER FOR ANY OTHER CONDITION

CLASS 3 SECTION 12408 VEHICLE CODE

x *Gary Chapman*

Right license:

EXPIRES ON BIRTHDAY IN **1986**

MD178563
Darlene Peterson
1843 Rose Ave.
Los Angeles, CA 90291

PRE LIC EXP

SEX	HAIR	EYES	HEIGHT	WEIGHT	
F	BRN	GRN	5-05½	120	80

DATE OF BIRTHDAY 12-24-48   MUST WEAR ☐ CORRECTIVE LENSES
OTHER ADDRESS   SEE OVER FOR ANY OTHER CONDITION

CLASS 3 SECTION 12408 VEHICLE CODE

x *Darlene Peterson*

Directions   Look at Gary and Darlene's driver's licenses above. Fill in the blank with the appropriate form of BE or BE + NOT.

examples   ___*Are*___ Darlene and Gary the same age?
(a)

No, they ___*aren't*___. Darlene ___*is*___ 32 years old and
(b) (c)

Gary ___*is*___ 37.
(d)

1. _____ Darlene's eyes green?
(a)

Yes, they _____, but Gary's eyes _____. His eyes _____ brown.
(b) (c) (d)

2. _____ Darlene and Gary tall? No, Darlene _____ tall. She _____ average. But
(a) (b) (c)

Gary _____ tall. He _____ 6'2" tall.
(d) (e)

3. _____ Darlene and Gary's eyes good? Yes, they _____. Darlene's
        (a)   (b)

eyes _____ 20/30, and Gary's eyes _____ 20/20.
        (c)   (d)

4. _____ Darlene's license good in 1987? No, it _____. It _____ good until 1986.
       (a)   (b)   (c)

5. _____ there pictures on the driver's licenses? Yes, there _____.
       (a)   (b)

6. _____ Darlene's hair brown? Yes, it _____. Gary's hair _____ brown too.
       (a)   (b)   (c)

EXERCISE #3. *IN/ON/AT.* LEVEL A.

Directions Fill in the blanks with IN, ON, or AT.

    example The typewriter is _____*on*_____ the desk.

    Ms. Olson is a secretary _____ the Housing Office _____ campus. The Housing
                              (1)   (2)

Office is _____ Dodd Hall, _____ room 79. Room 79 is _____ the basement.
        (3)   (4)   (5)

    Darlene and Chrissy are _____ line. Jonathan and Gary are _____ front of the
                              (6)   (7)

line, _____ the counter. The secretary is _____ her desk. She is _____ the phone.
    (8)   (9)   (10)

Name: _____ Date: _____

There are pencils _____ her cup and keys, paper clips, and a stapler _____ the desk.
(11)   (12)
There are cigarette butts _____ her ashtray. There's paper _____ the typewriter. There's
(13)   (14)
a sweater _____ the chair.
(15)

EXERCISE #4. *SOME/ANY.* LEVEL A.

Directions   Fill in the blanks with SOME or ANY.

    examples Are there _____*any*_____ new notices in the Housing Office?

                Yes, there are _____*some*_____ on the board.

Jonathan: What's that?

Gary: It's the local newspaper.

Jonathan: Are there _____ apartments for rent?
                       (1)

Gary: Sure . . . here on page four . . .

Jonathan: Are there _____ cheap apartments in Westwood?
                       (2)

Gary: No, there aren't _____ . They're all very expensive.
                           (3)

Jonathan: What about near the beach? Are there _____ cheap apartments near the beach?
(4)

Gary: Here are _____ in Venice. There are _____ one-bedroom apartments for rent,
(5)   (6)

but there aren't _____ two-bedroom apartments.
(7)

Jonathan: What about houses?

Gary: There are _____ houses in Santa Monica, but they're expensive.
(8)

Jonathan: Aren't there _____ in Venice?
(9)

Gary: No, there aren't, but there are _____ houses in Playa Del Rey and they're cheap!
(10)

Jonathan: Great!

EXERCISE #5. WRITING RULES. LEVEL A.

Directions Look at the information below. Then rewrite the information using capital letters, commas, periods, and apostrophes.

example dr bernstein is megs father
his first name is samuel
hes a doctor at a large hospital in chicago illinois

Dr. Bernstein is Meg's father. His first name is Samuel. He's a doctor at a large hospital in Chicago, Illinois.

1. mrs william peterson is a housewife in tamaqua pennsylvania
she has one son george
mrs peterson is darlenes mother
shes chrissys grandmother

_____

_____

_____

_____

2. miss linda moscowitz is jonathans sister
shes a graduate student at a large university in madison wisconsin
her address is 2109½ lakeside drive

_____

_____

_____

_____

Name: _____ Date: _____

3. mrs penny starsky is an architect in ithaca new york
   her husbands name is tom
   tom is bills brother
   hes an accountant for a large company IBM

   _____

   _____

   _____

   _____

   _____

4. lisa and craig smith have one son benjamin-john
   hes 1½ years old
   lisa is megs sister
   her home is in evanston illinois

   _____

   _____

   _____

   _____

EXERCISE #6. *THERE IS/THERE ARE.* LEVEL B.

Directions Describe the classroom. Write a sentence for each given noun using THERE IS or THERE ARE. Remember to use the indefinite article with singular count nouns.

   example projection screen: *There is a projection screen in the front of the classroom.*

1. blackboard: _____

2. tables: _____

3. windows: _____

4. door: _____

5. travel posters: _____

6. chairs: _____

7. desk: _____

8. clock: _____

9. wastepaper basket: _____

_____

10. books: _____

_____

11. cabinets: _____

12. light switch: _____

EXERCISE #7. QUESTIONS AND ANSWERS WITH *BE.* LEVEL B.

	GARY	DARLENE	JONATHAN
SEX	male	female	male
AGE	37 yrs.	32 yrs.	31 yrs.
HEIGHT	6' 2"	5' 5½"	5' 5"
HAIR COLOR	brown	brown	brown
OCCUPATION	teacher	student	student
EYE COLOR	brown	green	blue
COMPLEXION	fair	fair	dark

Directions a. Ask a question using the information given.
b. Answer the question. Use the short answer form.
c. Give the complete answer.

example Darlene and Jonathan/ teachers
a. *Are Darlene and Jonathan teachers ?*
b. *No, they aren't.*
c. *They're students.*

1. Gary and Jonathan/ female

a. _____

b. _____

c. _____

Name: _____ Date: _____

2. Gary and Jonathan/ 5' 4"

    a. _____

    b. _____

    c. _____

3. Darlene/ 32 years old

    a. _____

    b. _____

    c. _____

4. Darlene and Jonathan/ students

    a. _____

    b. _____

    c. _____

5. Jonathan/ fair

    a. _____

    b. _____

    c. _____

6. Gary's hair/ blond

    a. _____

    b. _____

    c. _____

7. Darlene and Jonathan's eyes/ brown

    a. _____

    b. _____

    c. _____

8. Gary and Darlene/ fair

    a. _____

    b. _____

    c. _____

EXERCISE #8. *IN/ON/AT.* LEVEL B.

Directions For each pair of nouns, write a sentence with the verb BE using IN, ON, or AT.

examples cup/desk *There is a cup on the desk.*

pens/cup *The pens are in the cup.*

1. student/ desk: _____

2. bookshelves/ wall: _____

3. books/ bookshelves: _____

4. wastepaper basket/ floor: _____

   _____

5. papers/ wastepaper basket: _____

   _____

6. plants/ desk: _____

7. pen/ Jonathan's hand: _____

8. clothes/ chair: _____

9. rug/ floor: _____

10. picture/ desk: _____

Name: _____ Date: _____ **67**

CLASSIFIED

apt. furnished

SUBLET—sunny Santa Monica. June 1. Quiet peaceful secure + separate entrance. 1 bdrm. apt.—Furnished + bath, shower & utilities included—5 minutes to beach. Gary 594-0628 $200.

FACULTY member has tiny guest house across from campus. Refrig hot plate. Prefer no car. $170; call 270-2340.

$315.00 unusually large well furnished 4 room/ 1 bth. Upper front 4 closets—new carpets—garage. Beverly Hills adjacent. 655-8217.

ONE bdrm sublease, furnished. Walk to school. $275/month. Call after 8 p.m. 377-3620.

3712 GAYLEY across from the dorms. Bachelors, singles, one bdrms. Call 472-8410.

FURNISHED/Unfurnished bachelor $175; singles $235, pool. Heart of Westwood. 804 Lindbrook. Call 775-5081.

BRENTWOOD—2 bdrms 2 bath air cond., luxury bldg., security garage. June 15–Dec. 15. $500 month. Only to persons able guarantee meticulous care—elegant new furnishings. 860-2791.

FURNISHED 1 bdrm summer rate or lease. $300 up. 806 Strathmore corner Landfair. Mgr #102.

PRIME Brentwood location, convenient shopping & transportation. Spacious singles furnished w/ full K & Ba. $265 & $275. Call 320-3225 or 481-8282.

apt. unfurnished

ONE OF A KIND STUDIO GUESTHOUSE IN WESTWOOD. WOOD BEAMS, SKYLIGHTS, FULL KITCHEN, STAINED GLASS. BRAND NEW. $395. CALL 493-4444.

SPACIOUS 2 Bd 2 Bth. A/C Fireplace·Double oven. Patio. Walk to Campus. $555.00 mo. Avail. immed. (714) 709-5337.

$285 1 bdrm, sunny, pool, clean, quiet, covered parking, drapes, carpets, appliances. Adults only. Mar Vista. 508-5600.

BACHELOR apt. $170.00 near City College. New carpet/paint. No cooking facilities. 477-0122.

house to share

SHARE quiet westside house, 10 mins bus. Prefer male grad. Available from June, 475-8110.

SHARE "bungalow" with yard, porch, hardwood floors with 1 other for summer. Close to school, beach. $125/mo. 887-7266.

house to rent

THREE bedroom furnished house available Jun 25–Sep 3. 15 minutes to campus. $400/mo. Faculty couple preferred. Day 805-6777. Eve 398-9606.

WESTWOOD—3 bdrm fireplace 1½ bath. Unfurnished. Appliances available. Lease, faculty. $550 (No pets) 474-5113.

SMALL 1 bdrm Santa Monica. Utilities. Furnished. Lease $375/month. Daniel X5-8210 after 4.

house to rent

MEDICAL school Prof. on sabbatical, spacious 4 bdrm fully furnished—15 min drive to campus. Available beg. Aug. for one year. No Sat. calls pls. Call 550-2726.

apt. to share

PEACEFUL, beautifully furnished large sunny apartment to share. 2 bedrooms, 2 baths in Brentwood. Call 826-9500 eves.

MALE wanted to share 1-bdrm apt westside near bus & grocery. 10 min. to beach nicely furnished. $140 + utilities starting mid-June. Call Jim 800-9308.

SUMMER roommate needed to share 1 bedroom Brentwood apt. Female, non-smoker only. Walk to shopping. $128.00. 870-7917 days or 498-8087 eves. Ask for Pam.

TWO mature women looking for third. Non-smoker, your own room, walk to campus. $135 plus utilities. Call evenings 470-0797.

Summer roommate (F)—one bdrm apt in Westwood. $137.50/mo. Swimming pool. Call 419-1213 day or night.

Male non-smoker wanted to share 3 bdrm apt in Westwood with 2 others. Grad preferred. Own bdrm. pool, sauna. Luxury bldg. $175.00 month. Call 474-7439.

EXERCISE #9. *SOME/ANY.* LEVEL B.

Directions Look at the Classified Ads above. Then answer the questions using SOME and ANY. Use the long answer form.

examples Are there any three-bedroom houses for rent?

Yes, there are some three-bedroom houses for rent.

Are there any houses to share in Beverly Hills?

No, there aren't any houses to share in Beverly Hills.

1. Are there any furnished bachelor apartments for rent?

_____

2. Are there any three-bedroom unfurnished apartments for rent?

_____

3. Are there any guest houses for rent near campus?

_____

4. Are there any apartments to share in Venice?

_____

5. Are there any two-bedroom apartments for rent for $200 a month?

_____

6. Are there any apartments to share in Brentwood?

_____

7. Are there any apartments with pools for rent?

_____

8. Are there any apartments within walking distance to campus?

_____

9. Are there any two-bedroom apartments for rent for $200 a month?

_____

10. Are there any two-bedroom houses for rent?

_____

EXERCISE #10.   PART I.   LEVEL C.

Directions Look at the picture and the vocabulary in the box below. Then read the model paragraph.

THINGS IN THE DRAWER	THINGS NOT IN THE DRAWER
pocket dictionary	paper clips
envelopes	rubber bands
eraser	thumb tacks
dark glasses	matches
scissors	scotch tape

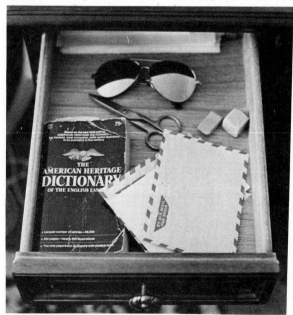

Name: _____   Date: _____

Model paragraph

There are many things in Gary's desk drawer. There is a pocket dictionary, an eraser, and envelopes. There are also scissors and dark glasses in his drawer. There aren't any paper clips, rubber bands, thumb tacks, or matches, and there isn't any scotch tape.

EXERCISE #10. PART II. LEVEL C.

Directions Look at the picture of Gary's desk. In the box below, make a list of the things on Gary's desk and the things not on Gary's desk. Then, using this vocabulary, write a paragraph describing the desk.

THINGS ON GARY'S DESK	THINGS NOT ON GARY'S DESK
_____	_____
_____	_____
_____	_____
_____	_____
_____	_____

Your paragraph

_____

_____

_____

_____

_____

_____

_____

_____

_____

_____

_____

_____

_____

_____

_____

_____

EXERCISE #11. PART I. LEVEL C.

Directions Look at the information in the box and read the following model dialogue.

INFORMATION ABOUT SANTA MONICA
near campus
nice area
close to the beach
good schools
quiet streets

Darlene: Hi, Meg?

Meg: Hi.

Darlene: This is Darlene. I'm at the Housing Office. There's a notice here about an apartment for rent in Santa Monica. Is Santa Monica near campus?

Meg: It's about five miles from school.

Darlene: Is it a nice area?

Meg: It's really nice. There's not much smog and it's quiet.

Darlene: Is it close to the beach?

Meg: Yes, it's on the coast.

Darlene: What about the schools? Are they good?

Meg: I think so. I don't really know.

Darlene: Are the streets busy?

Meg: No, not really . . . only Wilshire and Santa Monica Blvds.

Darlene: Okay, good. Thanks a lot, Meg.

Meg: Sure.

Darlene: Talk to you later. Bye.

Meg: Good-bye.

Name: _____ Date: _____

EXERCISE #11. PART II. LEVEL C.

Directions Write a dialogue between Meg and Darlene about Brentwood. Use the information in the box for Darlene's questions and Meg's answers.

```
┌────────────────────────────────────┐
│  INFORMATION ABOUT BRENTWOOD         │
├────────────────────────────────────┤
│         not much smog                │
│         not much traffic             │
│         nice neighborhood            │
│         expensive                    │
│         near shopping                │
│         close to campus              │
│         good schools                 │
└────────────────────────────────────┘
```

_____

_____

_____

_____

_____

_____

_____

_____

_____

_____

_____

_____

_____

_____

_____

_____

_____

EXERCISE #11. PART III. LEVEL C.

Directions Fill in the box with information about your neighborhood. Then write a dialogue between you and a friend. Answer your friend's questions about your neighborhood.

> INFORMATION ABOUT MY NEIGHBORHOOD
>
> _____
> _____
> _____
> _____
> _____
> _____
> _____
> _____
> _____
> _____

Name: _____ Date: _____

DECIDING TO LIVE TOGETHER

Outside the Housing Office

Jonathan: Are you new in Los Angeles?

Darlene: Yes, we are. We're living with friends in Pasadena, but Pasadena isn't close enough to campus. Are you new here too?

Gary: No, we're just looking for another apartment. We're living in Westwood now, but our apartment is too expensive and too small.

Jonathan: Yeah, it's a tiny one-bedroom apartment, and we're paying $425 a month.

Darlene: That's horrible! I'm a poor student and $425 is too expensive. Aren't there *any* cheap apartments near campus?

Gary: There are some, but not enough.

Darlene: What about near the beach? Are the apartments cheap?

Gary: They're usually cheap in Venice, but they're expensive in Santa Monica.

Darlene: Is Venice close to campus?

Jonathan: It's not too far from campus.

Darlene: My friends are living in a large house in Venice. They're moving out this weekend.

Jonathan: Whose house is it? Are they the owners?

Darlene: No, they aren't. They're renting it.

Jonathan: Is it expensive?
Darlene: The rent isn't too high, but the house is too big for two people. There are five bedrooms.
Jonathan: Hmm . . . but it's not too big for five people!
Darlene: Five people?
Chrissy: Yeah . . . you, Gary, Jonathan, me . . .
Darlene: . . . and maybe Meg.
Gary: . . . or our friend, Bill.
Darlene: That's not a bad idea. Let's have coffee and talk about it.
Jonathan: There's a cafeteria near this building. Let's go there.

THE PRESENT PROGRESSIVE

	We	are	going	to the market now.	
	My friends	are	moving	this weekend.	
	I	am	working	part-time this year.	
	Darlene	is	looking for	an apartment.	
Is	Jonathan		teaching	this semester?	No, he isn't.
Are	your friends		moving?		Yes, they are.
Are	they		standing	in line?	Yes, they are.
Is	your friend		waiting for	you?	Yes, he is.
Isn't	Gary		working	part-time this year?	No, he isn't.
Aren't	Darlene and Chrissy		going	to Europe next year?	No, they aren't.
Aren't	you		looking at	the notices?	Yes, I am.
Isn't	Meg		graduating	next year?	Yes, she is.
	I	am not	taking	chemistry this term.	
	He	isn't	standing	in line.	
	We	aren't	talking about	school.	
	My class	isn't	meeting	today.	

Notes

A. Form of the present progressive
  1. Positive statements: Use the present tense of the verb BE followed by the -ING form of the main verb.

$$BE + \underline{\quad}\text{-ING}$$
$$\text{(verb)}$$

  examples We're looking for an apartment.
  My friend is waiting in the cafeteria.

  2. Negative statements

$$BE + NOT + \underline{\quad}\text{-ING}$$
$$\text{(verb)}$$

  examples I'm not graduating this year.
  Chrissy isn't standing in line.

  3. Question form: BE or a contraction of BE plus NOT comes before the subject.

$$BE + (NOT) + \underline{\quad} + \underline{\quad}\text{-ING}$$
$$\text{(subject)} \quad \text{(verb)}$$

examples   Aren't you looking for an apartment?
Is your class meeting today?

4. Response: Long and short answers are possible, but short answers are more common.

QUESTION	SHORT ANSWER	LONG ANSWER
Is Chrissy standing in line?	No, she isn't.	No, she isn't standing in line.
Is Darlene standing in line?	Yes, she is.	Yes, she's standing in line.
Isn't Jonathan walking to school today?	Yes, he is.	Yes, he's walking to school today.
Isn't Gary walking to school today?	No, he isn't.	No, he isn't walking to school today.

a. You can give additional information after the YES or NO answer.

examples   Are you working full-time?
No, I'm a student.
Isn't your class meeting today?
No, the teacher's sick.
Are you going out tonight?
Yes, I'm meeting Ron at six.

5. Spelling rules
   a. Verbs ending with -E drop the -E before -ING.

take	taking
live	living
write	writing
have	having
give	giving
smoke	smoking

   b. When a verb ends with a short, stressed vowel before a consonant, double the consonant and add -ING.

sit	si*tt*ing
stop	sto*pp*ing
hit	hi*tt*ing
drop	dro*pp*ing
run	ru*nn*ing
swim	swi*mm*ing
prefér	prefe*rr*ing
forgét	forge*tt*ing

   c. Verbs ending with two consonants or with two vowels before a consonant do not change. Add -ING to the verb.

beat	beating
jump	jumping
heat	heating
stand	standing
look	looking
meet	meeting
rain	raining
eat	eating
drink	drinking
think	thinking

B. Use of the present progressive
  1. Use the present progressive to describe activities in progress.
    a. The present progressive shows that the activity is taking place now.

      examples   I'm drinking coffee.
                We're taking a break now.

    b. The activity in progress may extend over a period of time, but it always includes the present. Use the present progressive when the activity is temporary.

      examples   We're living in Pasadena right now.
                Darlene's looking for an apartment.

  2. Use the present progressive to talk about future activities.

      examples   They're moving *this weekend*.
                Next year Meg is graduating.

  3. Certain verbs are not used in the progressive form. (See Chapter Nine.)

WHOSE + *BE*

Whose is it?
  It's Jonathan's.
Whose house is it?
  It's my friends' house.
Whose apartment is this?
  It's my apartment.
Whose car is in the driveway?
  Darlene's.

Notes

A. The interrogative WHOSE asks about ownership or possession.
B. Position: In information questions, the interrogative WHOSE comes at the beginning of the sentence. Notice the similarity with YES/NO question word order.

  examples   ⎧ Is that Jonathan's motorcycle?
  Whose motorcycle ⎨ is that?
           ⎩
           ⎧ Is this Chrissy's?
      Whose ⎨ is this?
           ⎩

C. Form
  1. Pronoun form: WHOSE can be a pronoun. It takes the place of a noun.

      examples   Whose is this?
                Whose is that?

  2. Adjective form: WHOSE can be an adjective. It comes before a noun.

      examples   Whose car is in the driveway?
                Whose friends are living in Venice?

D. Responses: The answer to a WHOSE question usually has a possessive form.

      examples   *Whose* car is in the driveway?
                  Bill's.
                Whose room is this?
                  It's *my* room.
                Whose is this?
                  It's *Chrissy's.*

POSSESSIVE ADJECTIVES AND POSSESSIVE NOUNS. PART II.

Is your apartment near campus?
Our apartment is too small and too expensive.
Their house is in Venice.
Jonathan and Gary's apartment is in Westwood.
Darlene and Chrissy's home is in Pennsylvania.

Notes

A. Use: Possessive forms show ownership, possession, or close relationships.
B. Possessive nouns
   1. Add 'S to a singular noun to show possession. (See Chapter Two.)

      examples   That's the secretary's pen on the counter.
                    Jonathan's motorcycle is in the garage.

   2. With plural nouns ending in -S, add only an apostrophe (').

      examples   Students' schedules are very irregular.
                    Teachers' salaries are too low.

   3. With noun groups, the 'S is added to the last noun in the series.

      examples   Bill is Jonathan and Gary's friend.
                    Darlene and Chrissy's home is in Pennsylvania.

C. Possessive adjectives

	SINGULAR	PLURAL
1st person	my + _____ (noun)	our + _____ (noun)
2nd person	your + _____ (noun)	your + _____ (noun)
3rd person	$\begin{Bmatrix} his \\ her \\ its \end{Bmatrix}$ + _____ (noun)	their + _____ (noun)

      examples   Is *your* apartment a one-bedroom or a two-bedroom apartment?
                    Our apartment is tiny.

   1. The possessive adjective agrees in gender and number with the possessor. It does not agree with the noun it modifies.

Meg's brother ⬇ *Her* brother	A L S O	Meg's brothers ⬇ *Her* brothers
Jonathan's sister ⬇ *His* sister	A L S O	Jonathan's sisters ⬇ *His* sisters
Darlene and Meg's neighbor ⬇ *Their* neighbor	A L S O	Darlene and Meg's neighbors ⬇ *Their* neighbors

D. Double possessives: We sometimes use two possessive forms together.

    examples   *Her*   *grandmother's* furniture is antique.
                  (possessive (possessive
                    adjective)   noun)

                Jonathan's   *sister's*   husband is an engineer.
                (possessive (possessive
                noun)   noun)

E. A summary of possessive nouns and adjectives

		POSSESSIVE NOUN	POSSESSIVE ADJECTIVE
S		—	my + _____ (noun)
I		—	your + _____ (noun)
N **G** **U**		Bill's _____ (noun) the landlord's _____ (noun)	his + _____ (noun)
L **A**		Meg's _____ (noun) the landlady's _____ (noun)	her + _____ (noun)
R		the thing's _____ (noun)	its + _____ (noun)
P		Meg's and my _____ (noun)	our + _____ (noun)
L		Meg's and your _____ (noun)	your + _____ (noun)
U **R** **A** **L**		Gary and Jonathan's _____ (noun) Darlene and Chrissy's _____ (noun) Meg and Bill's _____ (noun) the students' _____ (noun)	their + _____ (noun)

AND/BUT/OR

    We're living in Pasadena now, but it's not close enough to campus.
    I'm living in a small apartment now, and the rent is $350.
    Are you working or going to school?
    I'm going to school part-time, and I'm working part-time.
    It's a nice house with five bedrooms, but it's too big for two people.

Notes

A. AND, BUT, and OR connect words, phrases, and sentences.
    1. AND
        a. Use AND to show an addition.

> **examples** The apartment is small and expensive.
> Jonathan is sitting in the cafeteria and talking with a friend.
> Venice isn't far from campus, and it's close to the beach.

b. Use AND before the last word or phrase in a series.

> **examples** There are five bedrooms, three bathrooms, a living room, a dining room, and a kitchen.
> Jonathan is sitting in the cafeteria, thinking about his term paper, and drinking coffee.

2. BUT
   a. Use BUT to show contrast.

> **examples** The apartment is small but expensive.
> It's dark in the living room but not in the kitchen.
> I'm not a student now, but I'm entering the university next semester.

b. BUT sometimes connects positive and negative sentences or phrases.

> **examples** Chrissy isn't hungry, but she's eating.
> Jonathan isn't at home but at school.

3. OR: Use OR to show an uncertainty or a choice.

> **examples** Is Bill a tennis teacher or a student?
> We're looking for an apartment near the beach or close to campus.
> Are there any cheap apartments, or are all of the apartments expensive?

B. A compound sentence is two or more sentences joined by AND, BUT, or OR.
   1. In compound sentences with two identical nouns, use a pronoun in place of the second noun.

> **examples** Is *Bill* a part-time student, or is *he* a a full-time student?
> (Bill)
> *Darlene* is a full-time student, and *she*'s working part-time.
> (Darlene)
> *Meg*'s major is business, but *she*'s also studying art.
> (Meg)

2. In compound sentences when the same subject and verb are repeated, you can omit the identical words in the second part of the sentence. The sentence that results is no longer called a compound sentence.

> **examples** We're living in a small apartment and (we are) paying $350 a month.
> There are five bedrooms and (there are) three baths.
> Are you living in Pasadena or (are you living) in Santa Monica?

C. Punctuation
   1. Commas separate words or phrases in a series.

> **examples** We're looking for an apartment in Venice, Santa Monica, or the Marina.
> There are five bedrooms, three bathrooms, a living room, a dining room, and a kitchen.
> They're going to the beach today, to the mountains tomorrow, and to the desert next week.

2. In a compound sentence, use a comma before AND, BUT, or OR.

> **examples** Adrienne's beautiful, but she's not dumb.
> We're living in a small apartment, and we're paying $350 a month.

LET'S IMPERATIVE

Let's go skiing this weekend.   Let's go to a movie.
Let's have coffee.   Let's not study tonight.

Notes

A. Form of the LET'S imperative
   1. Positive form: Use LET'S plus the base form of the verb.

$$\text{LET'S} + \underline{\hspace{2cm}}$$
$$\text{(verb)}$$

     examples   Let's go to a movie tonight.
                      Let's meet in the cafeteria.

   2. Negative form: Use NOT after LET'S to form the negative.

$$\text{LET'S} + \text{NOT} + \underline{\hspace{2cm}}$$
$$\text{(verb)}$$

     examples   Let's not cook dinner tonight.
                      Let's not eat at the cafeteria.

B. Meaning: The LET's imperative is an invitation or suggestion which includes the speaker and the listener(s).

C. LET'S GO: The -ING form of certain action verbs can come after LET'S GO.

$$\text{LET'S} + (\text{NOT}) + \text{GO} \underline{\hspace{2cm}} \text{-ING}$$
$$\text{(verb)}$$

LET'S GO. . .	
. . .swimming	. . .jogging
. . .skiing	. . .shopping
. . .hiking	. . .flying
. . .skating	. . .surfing
. . .sailing	. . .fishing
. . .running	. . .bowling
. . .dancing	. . .camping
. . .horseback riding	. . .bicycle riding

TOO/ENOUGH

We're living in Westwood now, but it's too expensive.
Venice isn't too far from campus.
We're staying in Pasadena now, but it isn't close enough to campus.
There aren't enough cheap apartments for rent.
We're renting a tiny one-bedroom apartment; it's big enough for one person, but it's too small for two people.

Notes

A. TOO shows an excessive amount or quality.

     examples   The desert is too hot in the summer. (I can't live there.)
                      This food is too salty. (I can't eat it.)
                      My coffee is too hot. (I can't drink it.)

   1. Position: TOO comes before an adjective or adverb.

$$\text{TOO} + \underline{\hspace{2.5cm}}$$
$$\text{(adjective or}$$
$$\text{adverb)}$$

examples   The exam is too *hard.*
(adjective)
You're speaking too *quickly.*
(adverb)

B. ENOUGH shows an adequate amount or degree.

examples   There's enough milk for breakfast.
Is your coffee hot enough?
Am I speaking slowly enough?

1. Position

a. ENOUGH can come before a noun phrase.

examples   Is there enough *time?*
(noun phrase)
There are enough *cheap apartments* in Venice.
(noun phrase)

b. ENOUGH can come after an adjective or adverb.

examples: Is the food *salty* enough?
(adjective)
Am I speaking *clearly* enough?
(adverb)

C. Negation
1. TOO: NOT TOO means something is not excessive.

examples   The food isn't too salty.
It isn't raining too hard.

2. ENOUGH: NOT ENOUGH shows that there isn't an adequate quality or quantity.

examples   Pasadena isn't close enough to campus.
There aren't enough minutes in a day.

3. Sentences with TOO and ENOUGH sometimes have similar meanings when they are used with adjectives or adverbs with opposite meanings.

NOT CLOSE ENOUGH = TOO FAR
NOT TOO EXPENSIVE = CHEAP ENOUGH

examples   Pasadena is too *far* from campus.
= It isn't *close* enough to campus.
The house isn't too *expensive.*
= It's *cheap* enough.

CONTRASTING ADJEC-TIVES		
fat	≠	thin
cheap	≠	expensive
big	≠	small
short	≠	tall
close	≠	far
cold	≠	hot
light	≠	heavy
dark	≠	light
wet	≠	dry
clean	≠	dirty

EXERCISE #1. THE PRESENT PROGRESSIVE. PART I. LEVEL A.

Directions Fill in the blanks with the proper form of the verb BE.

    example Chrissy ____*is*____ standing in line.

1.   Jonathan and Gary _____ looking for an apartment. They _____ living near campus
                      (1)   (2)
now, but they _____ paying $425 a month for rent.
                    (3)
      Right now they _____ standing outside Dodd Hall. Gary _____ playing with Chrissy,
                        (4)   (5)
and Jonathan _____ talking to Darlene. They _____ talking about the housing lists.
                    (6)   (7)

2.   I _____ studying English at the university. Right now, we _____ not studying because
          (1)   (2)
we _____ taking a break. Several students _____ sitting on the stairs. They _____
      (3)   (4)   (5)

Name: _____ Date: _____ **85**

drinking coffee. I _____ not drinking coffee, but I _____ smoking a cigarette. The
                        (6)   (7)

teacher _____ talking to a student about his homework assignment.
            (8)

EXERCISE #1. THE PRESENT PROGRESSIVE. PART II. LEVEL A.

Directions Fill in the blanks with the present progressive form of the given verb. Use
BE + _____ -ING.
        (verb)

    example Jonathan ___*is standing*___ at the counter.
                    STAND

1.   Darlene, Chrissy and Gary _____ in the cafeteria.
                                  (1) SIT

    Darlene and Gary _____ coffee, and they _____ apart-
                        (2) DRINK   (3) TALK ABOUT

ments. Chrissy _____ a hamburger, and she _____ all
                      (4) EAT   (5) LOOK AT

the people. Jonathan _____ a cup of coffee. He _____
                        (6) GET   (7) BUY

a sandwich too. Now he _____ in line. The woman in front of Jonathan
                      (8) STAND

_____. She _____ change.
    (9) PAY   (10) WAIT FOR

2. *Darlene:* My friends _____ in a big house in Venice.
(1) LIVE

They _____ this weekend.
(2) MOVE

Jonathan: _____ they _____ much rent?
(3) PAY

Darlene: They _____ only $750 a month.
(4) PAY

Jonathan: _____ they _____ because they
(5) MOVE

_____ problems with the landlord?
(6) HAVE

Darlene: No, they aren't. The landlord is real nice. They _____
(7) START

a new program this semester at the University of Michigan.

Jonathan: _____ you _____ into their house?
(8) MOVE

Darlene: I don't know. We _____ more people.
(9) LOOK FOR

EXERCISE #2. INTERROGATIVES: *WHO/ WHAT/ WHOSE.* LEVEL A.

Directions Fill in the blanks with WHO, WHAT, or WHOSE.

example *Chrissy:* ___*What*___'s this?

Darlene: It's a plant hanger.

Darlene: Let's look through this stuff and organize it. I'm sure Sue and Jeff are tired of this mess in their garage. Let's get some boxes and repack.

Chrissy: Is this box okay?

Name: _____ Date: _____

Darlene: No . . . maybe that box in the corner.

Chrissy: _____'s wrong with this box?
              (1)

Darlene: It's too small.

Chrissy: Oh, okay. _____'s this?
                      (2)

Darlene: It's an old coffee maker.

Chrissy: It's funny looking. _____ is it?
                           (3)

Darlene: It's Sue's.

Chrissy: Oh, look . . . a photo album. _____ is it?
                                  (4)

Darlene: That's my album, Chrissy.

Chrissy: _____ is the man in this picture?
              (5)

Darlene: That's my cousin, Paul.

Chrissy: Is that his car?

Darlene: Mm . . . hmm. . .

Chrissy: _____ kind is it?
              (6)

Darlene: I think it's a 1955 Chevy.

Chrissy: Mommy, _____'s this man?
                  (7)

Darlene: That's an old boyfriend.
        Let's repack this box.

Chrissy: _____'s in it?
              (8)

Darlene: Old clothes.

Chrissy: _____ nightgown is this?
              (9)

Darlene: It's my nightgown.

Chrissy: Yick, it's ugly.

Darlene: Yeah, let's throw it away.

Chrissy: Good idea.

Darlene: Is that car coming into this driveway?

Chrissy: Yeah.

Darlene: _____ is it?
              (10)

Chrissy: It's Jeff.

Darlene: He's home early today. Let's stop this and talk to Jeff.

EXERCISE #3. POSSESSIVE ADJECTIVES. LEVEL A.

Directions Fill in the blank with MY, YOUR, HIS, HER, ITS, OUR, *or* THEIR.

example   *Gary:* Is ___*your*___ apartment a one-bedroom or a two-bedroom, Bill?

Bill: It's a one-bedroom.

Gary: Hi, Bill. This is Gary.

Bill: Hi, Gary. What's happening?

Gary: Well, Jon and I are still looking at apartments.

Bill: Still? What's the problem?

Gary: Everything's too expensive.

Bill: I know. _____ place is too expensive too. I'm paying $450 a month for a one-bedroom.
        (1)

Gary: Yeah, Jon and I are paying $425 now for _____ tiny one-bedroom.
                                                (2)

Bill: Are you looking only in Westwood?

Gary: No, we're looking near the beach. There's an ad in today's paper for an apartment in Venice. We're also looking at houses.

Bill: Houses!! They're *really* expensive!

Gary: Well, there are two other people. They're also looking for a place. With four or five people, a house isn't too expensive.

Bill: And *who* are these other people?

Gary: Well, there's this woman and _____ daughter. They're living in Pasadena right now,
                                       (3)

but _____ place is too far from campus.
       (4)

Bill: Who's this woman?

Gary: A student at the university. She's from Pennsylvania. I think she's studying Political Science.

Bill: What's _____ name?
                  (5)

Name: _____   Date: _____   **89**

Gary: Darlene . . . Darlene Peterson.

Bill: Are you and Jon *sure* this is a good idea?

Gary: Oh, yeah. Jon and I are excited about the idea of a house. We're really tired of _____

(6)

small apartment. Actually, that's the reason I'm calling. Are *you* interested in the idea?

Bill: Well, I'm not sure about the kid. What's _____ name?

(7)

Gary: Chrissy.

Bill: Is she okay?

Gary: Yeah, she's a typical kid . . . maybe a bit too active. . .

Bill: Hmm. . . .

Gary: Well, Bill, what's _____ answer. Yes or no?

(8)

Bill: It's a possibility. _____ rent is really too high here, but the apartment is nice. I'm really

(9)

not sure. Let me think about it and call you tomorrow. Okay?

Gary: Sure.

Bill: Is _____ number the same?

(10)

Gary: Yeah, it's still 573-3790.

Bill: Okay . . . talk to you tomorrow. Are you home after five?

Gary: Yeah . . . talk to you then.

Bill: Bye.

EXERCISE #4. *AND/BUT/OR.* LEVEL A.

Directions Fill in the blanks with the conjunctions AND, BUT, or OR.

    example *Darlene:* Are you having lunch now ___*or*___ just a snack?
                Meg: I'm having lunch.

Darlene: Am I late?

Meg: No, not at all.

Darlene: What are you drinking? Is that a gin and tonic _____ a Vodka Collins?
(1)

Meg: It's a gin and tonic.

Darlene: I'm really thirsty, _____ I'm starving too.
(2)

Meg: There's the waitress. She's bringing the menu.

Darlene: Great.

Waitress: Hi! Are you having lunch _____ just cocktails?
(3)

Darlene: Let's see. Bring me a Bloody Mary, please, _____ let me see the lunch menu.
(4)

Waitress: Okay, Here's the menu. I'll bring your drink right away.

Darlene: Thanks. Hmm. . . . there's a big selection.

Meg: The pizza here is great.

Darlene: Yeah, pizza's always good, _____ it's too fattening.
(5)

Meg: There's a combination plate with soup _____ half a sandwich.
(6)

Darlene: It's probably good, _____ it's not filling enough.
(7)

Meg: Well, what about a whole sandwich _____ a small dinner salad?
(8)

Darlene: Hmm . . . here's a seafood salad. It comes with French bread _____ whipped butter.
(9)

Waitress: Here's your Bloody Mary. Are you ready to order?

Darlene: Yes, I'll have the seafood salad _____ coffee.
(10)

Waitress: What kind of dressing? . . . French, Thousand Island, Italian, Roquefort, _____ herb?
(11)

Darlene: Herb dressing, please.

Waitress: Do you want the coffee with your meal, _____ after your meal?
(12)

Darlene: With, please.

Meg: So, let's hear all about your apartment search.

Darlene: Oh, that's a long story. . .

EXERCISE #5. *TOO/ENOUGH.* LEVEL A.

Directions Complete the sentences below with one of the following patterns.

    a. TOO + _____
          (adjective)

    b. _____ + ENOUGH
          (adjective)

example hard: The bed is *too hard*.
          soft: It isn't *soft enough*.

Name: _____ Date: _____

1.

   a. long: The car is _____.
   b. short: It isn't _____.

2.

   a. tall: She isn't _____.
   b. short: She's _____.

3.

   a. quiet: Park Avenue isn't _____
      _____.
   b. noisy: It's _____.

4.

   a. easy: This test isn't _____.
   b. difficult: It is _____.

5.

   a. cold: It's _____
      in Alaska.
   b. warm: It isn't _____.

6.

a. hot: This coffee is _____ .

b. cool: It isn't _____ .

7.

a. dark: The room is _____ .

b. light: It isn't _____ .

8.

a. small: The shoe is _____ .

b. big: It isn't _____ .

EXERCISE #6.   THE PRESENT PROGRESSIVE.   LEVEL B.

Directions   Write a sentence with the information given. Use the present progressive.

example   What is Darlene doing?

1. stand / in line: *Darlene is standing in line.*

2. wait: *She's waiting.*

Name: _____   Date: _____

1.

What is Darlene doing?

a. get / a cup of coffee: _____

_____

b. pay / the cashier: _____

_____

c. go / to the table: _____

_____

d. sit / at the table: _____

_____

2.

What is Chrissy doing?

a. wait for / Darlene: _____

_____

b. talk / to Jonathan and Gary: _____

_____

c. eat / her hamburger: _____

_____

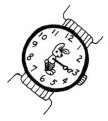

d. drink / her coke: _____

_____

3.

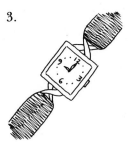

What are Meg and Darlene doing?

a. drive / to school: _____

_____

b. study / at the library: _____

_____

c. go / to class: _____

_____

d. sit / in the cafeteria: _____

_____

Name: _____ Date: _____

EXERCISE #7. INTERROGATIVES: *WHO/WHAT/WHOSE.* LEVEL B.

Directions   Write a question with WHO, WHOSE, or WHAT.

example   *Darlene:* <u>Who's this</u>?
            Chrissy: It's my friend.
            Darlene: <u>What's his name</u>?
            Chrissy: Teddy.

Chrissy: I'm showing the house to my friend, Teddy. Is that okay?
Darlene: Sure, but be quiet. Sue's sleeping.
Chrissy: Okay.

Teddy: _____?
                              (1)

Chrissy: Sue is a friend. We're just staying with Sue and Jeff. We're looking for an apartment.
Teddy: Who's Jeff?
Chrissy: Sue's husband.

Teddy: _____?
                              (2)

Chrissy: He's an architect.

Teddy: _____?
                              (3)

Chrissy: It's Jeff's study.

Teddy: _____?
                              (4)

Chrissy: It's a drafting table.

Teddy: _____?
                              (5)

Chrissy: Sue's an accountant.
Teddy: Wow, what a lot of books in here.

            _____?
                              (6)

Chrissy: They're Mommy's books. She's a student.
Teddy: Let's go outside.
Chrissy: Okay, let's go out front. Jeff's coming home soon.

EXERCISE #8. POSSESSIVE NOUNS AND POSSESSIVE ADJECTIVES. LEVEL B.

Directions Write sentences using the possessive forms to show the relationships between the people below.
   a. Use the possessive noun form.
   b. Use the possessive adjective form.

   example Chrissy/ Darlene/ daughter
   a. *Chrissy is Darlene's daughter.*
   b. *Chrissy is her daughter.*

1. Darlene/ Chrissy/ mother

   a. _____

   b. _____
2. Meg/ Darlene and Chrissy/ friend

   a. _____

   b. _____
3. Jon and Gary/ Bill/ friends

   a. _____

   b. _____
4. Mr. and Mrs. Starsky/ Bill/ parents

   a. _____

   b. _____
5. Meg/ the Bernsteins/ daughter

   a. _____

   b. _____
6. Ms. Gladstone/ Chrissy/ piano teacher

   a. _____

   b. _____
7. Jimmy, Elaine, Tom, and Fred/ Gary/ students

   a. _____

   b. _____
8. Muffin/ Mr. Garvey/ dog

   a. _____

   b. _____

EXERCISE #9. *AND/BUT/OR.* LEVEL B.

Direction Combine the following sentences using AND, OR, or BUT. Omit identical elements when possible. Use a pronoun in place of the second identical noun.

   example Are you looking for an apartment? Are you looking for a house?

   Are you looking for an apartment or a house?

   1. There are lots of apartments near campus. There aren't any apartments for rent.

   _____

Name: _____   Date: _____

2. Are you working part-time? Are you working full-time?

_____

3. The bedrooms are very tiny. There is a large living room.

_____

4. I need a large apartment. I need a small house.

_____

5. There are seven bedrooms. There is only one bathroom.

_____

6. Is the apartment close to the beach? Is the apartment far from the beach?

_____

7. The kitchen is large. There are a lot of cupboards.

_____

8. I like Pasadena. Pasadena is too far from campus.

_____

9. In the kitchen there is a dishwasher. There is a stove. There is a refrigerator. There is an oven.

_____

10. I'm living too far from campus now. I'm paying too much rent.

_____

EXERCISE #10. *LET'S.* LEVEL B.

Directions Look at the pictures. Then write a sentence using LET'S or LET'S NOT.

examples

Let's go bicycle riding .

Let's not watch television .

1.

_____ .

2.

_____ .

3.

_____ .

4.

_____ .

5.

_____ .

6.

_____ .

7.

_____ .

8.

_____ .

Name: _____ Date: _____

EXERCISE #11. *TOO/ENOUGH.* LEVEL B.

Directions Write two sentences using the given subject. Use the adjectives and the modifiers TOO and ENOUGH.

example   smart / dumb   1. Chrissy *isn't smart enough* .
2. *She's too dumb* .

1.

polite / rude

a. Chrissy _____ .

b. _____ .

2.

poor / rich

a. I _____ .

b. _____ .

3.

soft / loud

a. The music _____ .

b. _____ .

4.

weak / strong

a. You _____ .

b. _____ .

100

5.

dirty / clean

a. His hands _____ .

b. _____ .

6.

easy / hard

a. This lesson _____ .

b. _____ .

7.

young / old

a. The child _____ .

b. _____ .

8.

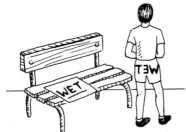

dry / wet

a. The paint _____ .

b. _____ .

9.

happy / sad

a. She _____ .

b. _____ .

Name: _____ Date: _____

10.

high / low

a. Her heels _____ .

b. _____ .

EXERCISE #12.   LEVEL C.

Directions   Answer the question using the present progressive.

example   What are you doing?

I'm eating breakfast. _____

_____

I'm going to work. _____

_____

This is the time.	What are you doing?	
		M O R N I N G

This is the time.	What are you doing?	
		A F T E R N O O N
		E V E N I N G

EXERCISE # 13.   PART I.   LEVEL C.

Directions   Read the dialogue between Darlene and Mr. Jones.

Darlene: Are you Mr. Jones?

Landlord: Yes, I am.

Darlene: Is there an apartment for rent in your building?

Landlord: Yes, there are two apartments for rent.

Darlene: I'm looking for a small apartment.

Landlord: There's a one-bedroom apartment for rent. It's small, but it's very nice.

Darlene: Is the rent high?

Landlord: It's $250 a month.

Darlene: Is there a deposit or a cleaning fee?

Landlord: Yes, there's a $50 deposit and a $30 cleaning fee.

Darlene: Where is the apartment?

Landlord: It's in Venice on Washington Boulevard near Lincoln.

Darlene: That's too far. I'm a student at the university, and I'm looking for an apartment near campus. Thank you.

Landlord: You're welcome.

EXERCISE # 13.   PART II. LEVEL C.

Directions   Write a dialogue between you and Mrs. Smith.
Ask about the apartment for rent.

_____

_____

_____

_____

_____

_____

_____

_____

_____

_____

_____

_____

_____

LET'S HAVE COFFEE

At the cafeteria

Gary: Okay, Jon. Let's hear your idea.

Jonathan: Well, the house in Venice has five bedrooms, and there are four of us . . . with five people a house really isn't more expensive than an apartment.

Darlene: That's true. I think the rent is only $750 a month.

Jonathan: Let's see. That's $150 apiece with five people. That's cheaper than our apartment. We're paying over $200 a month each now, without utilities.

Darlene: Chrissy and I are sharing a bedroom now. With my salary $150 a month apiece is too expensive.

Chrissy: One bedroom is really big enough.

Gary: Okay, that's three bedrooms . . . you and Chrissy have one, and Jonathan and I each have our own. Let's find two more people.

Jonathan: What about Bill?

Gary: Why Bill? He has a nice apartment in the Marina.

Jonathan: Yeah, but his apartment is expensive. Besides, a house is always nicer.

Darlene: Who's Bill?

Gary: He's our ex-neighbor. He's working in the Marina now as a tennis teacher.

Darlene: What's he like?

Gary: He's outgoing and athletic. He has blond hair and blue eyes.

Jonathan:	He's a real ladies' man.
Darlene:	How old is he?
Gary:	I don't know. He's younger than Jon . . . about 27 or 28.
Darlene:	Is he nice?
Gary:	Sure, he's a really nice guy. He's very easy to get along with.
Jonathan:	What about your friend, Meg?
Chrissy:	Yeah, Mom, let's ask Meg. She's great!
Darlene:	That's an idea. She's looking for an apartment too.
Jonathan:	What's she like?
Darlene:	She's 26, pretty, and very active.
Gary:	Is she a student?
Darlene:	Yes, she's a graduate student in the School of Management, and she has a part-time job as a secretary. She's easy to get along with too.
Gary:	Okay, let's ask Meg and Bill.

HAVE: PRESENT TENSE STATEMENT FORM

THIRD PERSON SINGULAR FORM	OTHER FORMS
Meg *has* a part-time job. She *has* a job as a secretary. The house *has* five bedrooms. He *has* blond hair. Bill *has* an expensive apartment.	I *have* an idea. We *have* a friend. You *have* a daughter. Gary and Jonathan *have* an apartment in Westwood. Meg and Darlene *have* dark hair.

Notes

A. Form: HAVE is an irregular verb.
B. Meaning
   1. The verb HAVE sometimes shows possession.

   examples   Gary has an old car.
                Meg and Darlene have a lot of clothes.

   2. Other expressions with HAVE.

EXPRESSIONS WITH *HAVE*

HAVE ⎰ BREAKFAST
⎱ LUNCH
   DINNER
   A DRINK
	Meg has breakfast at 7 A.M.
	Let's have a drink.	

HAVE + _____ (name of an illness)	Chrissy has a cold. Jonathan has the flu.	
HAVE + _____ + _____ (adjective) (body part)	Darlene has long hair. Bill has blue eyes.	
HAVE A JOB AS A + _____ (occupation)	I have a job as a carpenter. Darlene's friend has a job as a waitress.	

HAVE A {PART-TIME / FULL-TIME} JOB	Gary and Bill have full-time jobs. Meg has a part-time job.
HAVE A FRIEND	I have a friend in Dallas, Texas. Darlene has some friends in Venice.
HAVE A + _____ (relative)	Gary has a sister in Oregon. Meg has an aunt in France.
HAVE AN IDEA	I have an idea—let's live together. Jonathan has a great idea—we can rent the house in Venice.
HAVE TIME	Jonathan never has time for lunch. Meg has time for grocery shopping tomorrow.
HAVE A {GOOD / BAD} TIME	We always have a good time at the beach. Jonathan has a bad time at parties.
HAVE A PARTY	We're having a house-warming party. Chrissy's having a birthday party.
HAVE THE USE OF	Meg has the use of her boyfriend's car. Darlene has the use of her friends' swimming pool.

Parts of the body

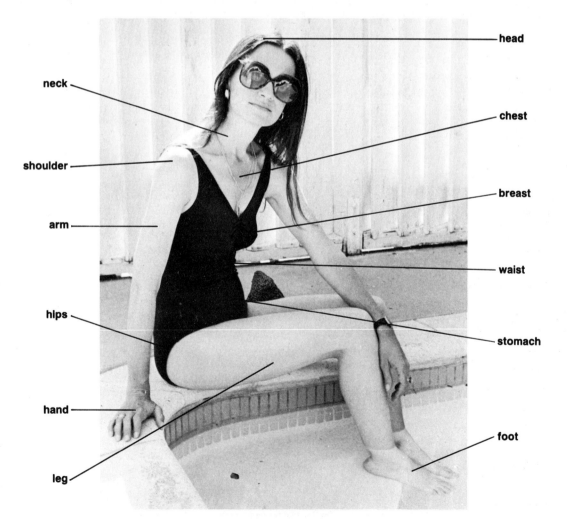

neck · shoulder · arm · hips · hand · leg · head · chest · breast · waist · stomach · foot

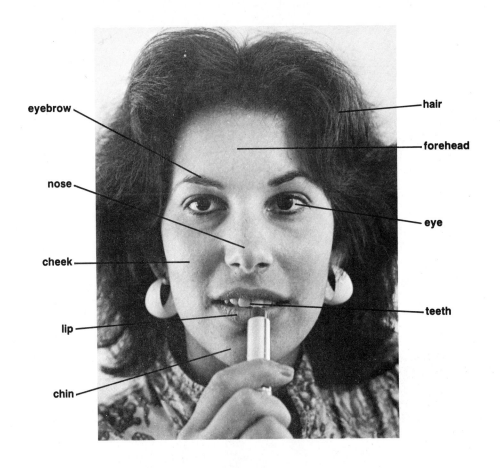

eyebrow

hair

forehead

nose

eye

cheek

teeth

lip

chin

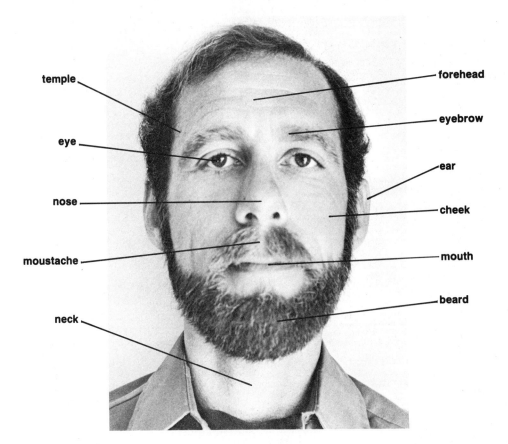

temple

forehead

eyebrow

eye

ear

nose

cheek

moustache

mouth

beard

neck

Arm

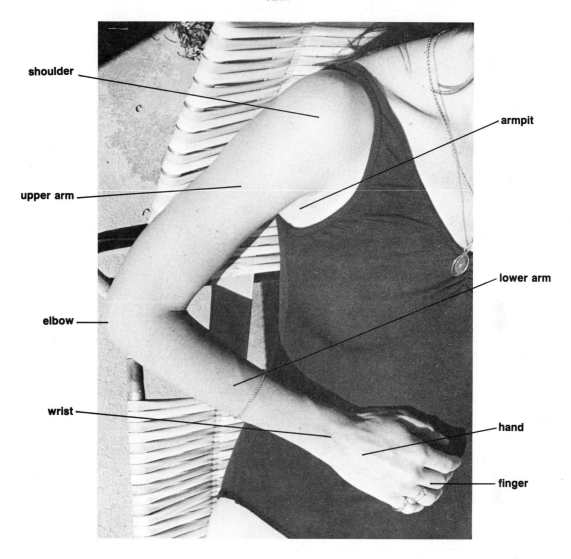

shoulder

armpit

upper arm

lower arm

elbow

wrist

hand

finger

Leg

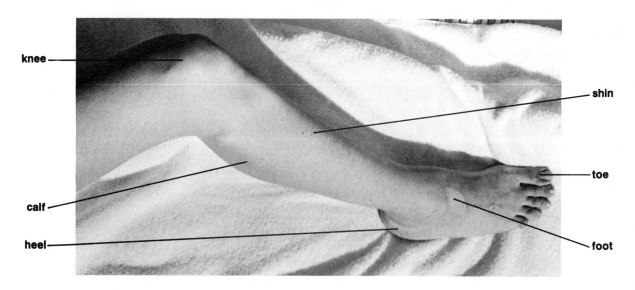

knee

shin

calf

toe

heel

foot

Hand

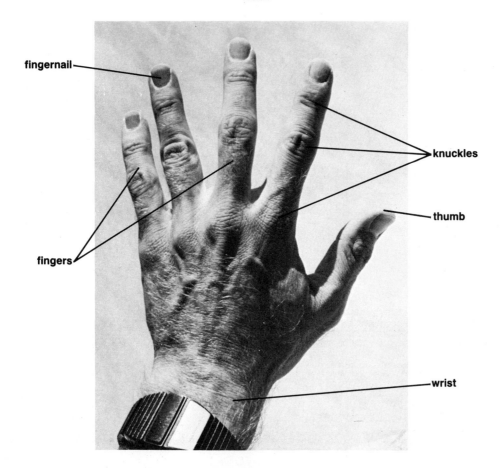

fingernail

knuckles

thumb

fingers

wrist

Foot

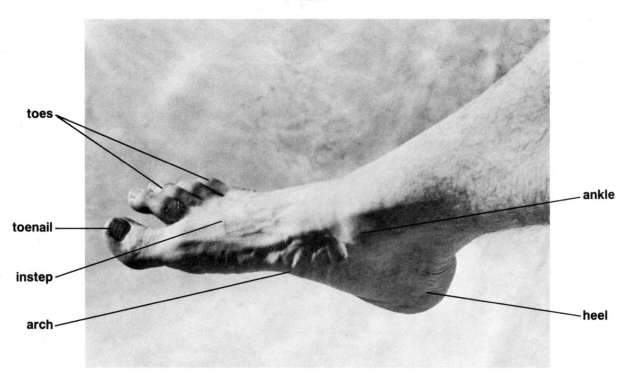

toes

ankle

toenail

instep

arch

heel

110

PARTS OF THE BODY

Notes

A. Singular/plural noun forms (See Chapter One.)
   1. Regular noun plurals

Pronunciation of Plural Endings

/s/		/z/		/ɪz/	
lip cheek wrist	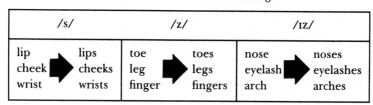 lips cheeks wrists	toe leg finger	toes legs fingers	nose eyelash arch	noses eyelashes arches

   2. Irregular noun plurals

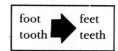

foot → feet
tooth → teeth

examples Darlene has big feet.
Gary has strong teeth.

B. Mass nouns: We do not use plural forms with mass nouns. (See Chapter One.)

examples My hair is long. I have long hair.

My skin is fair. 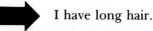 I have fair skin.

C. Possessives: Use a possessive adjective or possessive noun with parts of the body.

examples *My* hair is dry.
His feet are big.
Meg's hair is curly.

   1. The possessive adjective does not usually occur after HAVE and before the name of a part of the body, since HAVE indicates a degree of possession.

examples My hair is dry. I have dry hair.

His feet are big. He has big feet.

Meg's hair is curly. Meg has curly hair.

```
┌──────────────────────────────────────────────────────────────────┐
│              HUMAN PHYSICAL QUALITIES: ADJECTIVES                   │
├──────────────────────────────────────────────────────────────────┤
```

BODY SIZE	*APPEARANCE*	
	Male	*Female*
short/tall	handsome	beautiful
fat/thin	good-looking	pretty
plump/skinny	cute	cute
overweight/underweight	nice-looking	nice-looking
average	ugly	ugly

AGE	*HANDS*	*FEET*
old/young	big/small	big/small
middle-aged		narrow/wide
		flat

EYE COLOR	*EYE SIZE*	*VISION*
blue	big/small	20–20 = perfect
green		nearsighted/farsighted
hazel		
brown		
dark		

		COMPLEXION
HAIR COLOR	*HAIR QUALITY*	*QUALITY*
blond	oily/dry	clear = good
black	normal	bad
brown	long/short	poor
red	shoulder-length	fair = light
grey	straight	dark
white	wavy	olive
light/dark	curly	
	frizzy	

TEETH	*NOSE*	*NECK*
white/yellow	big/small	thick/slender
crooked/straight	thin	long/short
good/bad	long	
	cute	
	button	
	turned-up	
	straight/ hooked	

ADJECTIVES: COMPARATIVE FORMS

> That's cheaper than our apartment.
> A house really isn't more expensive than an apartment.
> Besides, a house is always nicer.
> He's younger than Jonathan . . . about 27 or 28.

Notes

A. Use: The comparative form of an adjective expresses differences between two things, persons, or ideas.

    examples   Chrissy is younger than Darlene.

               young
CHRISSY ————————> DARLENE

Jonathan is shorter than Gary.

$$\text{JONATHAN} \xrightarrow{\text{short}} \text{GARY}$$

1. The items compared may be singular or plural.

   examples   *Bill* is younger than *Gary.*
                      Bill is younger than *Gary, Jonathan,* and *Darlene.*

                      New York is larger than *Chicago.*
                      New York and Chicago are larger than *Philadelphia, Boston,* and *Washington, D.C.*

2. When both elements of the comparison are expressed, the comparative form of the adjective is followed by THAN.

$$\underset{\text{(element 1)}}{\underline{\qquad\qquad}} + \underset{\text{(verb)}}{\underline{\qquad}} + \underset{\substack{\text{(comparative}\\\text{adjective)}}}{\underline{\qquad\qquad}} + \text{THAN} + \underset{\text{(element 2)}}{\underline{\qquad\qquad}}$$

   examples   Gary is more practical than Meg.
                      Apartments in Venice are cheaper than apartments in Beverly Hills.

B. Form of the comparative
   1. With one-syllable adjectives, add -ER to most adjectives to form the comparative

$$\underset{\text{(adjective)}}{\underline{\qquad\qquad}}\text{-ER}$$

   a. The final consonant is doubled when it comes after a single vowel.

BASE FORM	COMPARATIVE FORM
short	shorter
tall	taller
old	older
young	younger

but

BASE FORM	COMPARATIVE FORM
big	bi*gg*er
fat	fa*tt*er
hot	ho*tt*er
thin	thi*nn*er

   examples   Gary is bigger than Jonathan.
                      Darlene is older than Meg.

   b. Add -ER to two-syllable adjectives ending in -Y, -OW, or -ER. -Y changes to -I before -ER.

BASE FORM	COMPARATIVE FORM
narrow	narrower
shallow	shallower
clever	cleverer
slender	slenderer

but

BASE FORM	COMPARATIVE FORM
happy	happ*i*er
busy	bus*i*er

2. In most other cases, the comparative form of the adjective is MORE or LESS plus the adjective.

MORE >
LESS <

BASE FORM		COMPARATIVE FORM
careful polite honest	→	more careful more polite more honest
intelligent beautiful serious	→	more intelligent more beautiful more serious

examples   Bill is *more athletic* than Darlene.
Darlene is *less athletic* than Bill.

3. For some adjectives, the comparative form is irregular.

BASE FORM		COMPARATIVE FORM
good bad	→	better worse
{much many}	→	more
little	→	less

examples   Darlene's sunburn is *worse* than Meg's.
Bill's tennis game is *better* than Gary's.

HAVE/BE

     This is Cindy. She's young. She's short and skinny. She has glasses and freckles. Her teeth are crooked, and she has braces. Her hair is long, straight, and red. She has braids.

This is Henry. He's tall and thin. He's bald, and he has glasses. His eyes are brown, and he's nearsighted.

This is Mabel. She's old, and she has wrinkles. Her hair is white and frizzy. She's skinny and tiny.

This is Francis. He's tall and well built. He has muscles. His hair is curly and dark. He has a beard and a moustache. He also has glasses.

This is Kathleen. She's young. She has beautiful long, blond hair. Her nose is small and thin. Her complexion is fair. She has a good figure. Her eyes are blue. Her teeth are white and straight. She has a nice smile.

This is Violet. She's short and plump. She is middle-aged. Her eyes are green, and her hair is blond. She has short, curly hair.

HAVE/BE

He's outgoing and athletic.
He has blond hair and blue eyes.
How old is he?
    About 27 or 28.
She's 26, pretty and very active.

Notes

A. There is no single rule for predicting the use of HAVE and BE in descriptive expressions.
B. BE: The verb BE can come before an adjective.

    examples Her eyes are *big*.
                      (adjective)
          Jonathan is *nearsighted*.
                    (adjective)

```
┌─────────────────────────────┐
│  Expressions with BE        │
├─────────────────────────────┤
│  She's pretty.              │
│  He's handsome.             │
│  She's short and fat.       │
│  He's tall and thin.        │
│  She's old.                 │
│  He's young.                │
│  I'm 22 years old.          │
│  He's bald.                 │
│  He's nearsighted.          │
└─────────────────────────────┘
```

C. HAVE: The verb HAVE comes before a noun phrase.

    examples   She has *big eyes.*
                         (noun phrase)
              He has *blond hair.*
                         (noun phrase)

```
┌──────────────────────────────────────┐
│       Expressions with HAVE          │
├──────────────────────────────────────┤
│  She has ⎰braids.      ⎱              │
│          ⎱a pony tail. ⎰              │
│  He has a good build.                │
│  She has braces.                     │
│  He has brown eyes.                  │
│  She has wrinkles.                   │
│  She has freckles.                   │
│  I have pimples.                     │
│  He has a moustache and a beard.     │
│  He has glasses.                     │
└──────────────────────────────────────┘
```

D. Some characteristics can be expressed either with BE or HAVE. Notice the similarity in meaning in the sentences below.

    examples   Her eyes are big.   She has big eyes.

                  His hair is blond.   He has blond hair.

```
┌────────────────────────────────────────────────────────────┐
│                 Expressions with BE and HAVE               │
├────────────────────────────────────────────────────────────┤
│  Her eyes are green.           She has green eyes.         │
│  Her hair is blond.            She has blond hair.         │
│  Her hair is straight.         She has straight hair.      │
│  Her nose is big.              She has a big nose.         │
│  My teeth are white.           I have white teeth.         │
│       ⎰complexion⎱                    ⎰a good complexion.⎱  │
│  His  ⎱skin      ⎰ is good.    He has ⎱good skin.        ⎰  │
│       ⎰complexion⎱                    ⎰a fair complexion.⎱  │
│  Her  ⎱skin      ⎰ is fair.    She has⎱fair skin.        ⎰  │
│  Her eyes are big.             She has big eyes.           │
│  My feet are small.            I have small feet.          │
│  Her figure is good.           She has a good figure.      │
└────────────────────────────────────────────────────────────┘
```

OR

Adjectives of nationality

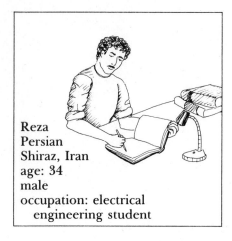

Reza
Persian
Shiraz, Iran
age: 34
male
occupation: electrical
   engineering student

Fred
American
Kansas City,
   Kansas
age: 26
male
occupation: librarian

Elizabeth
English
Bath, England
age: 16
female
occupation: waitress

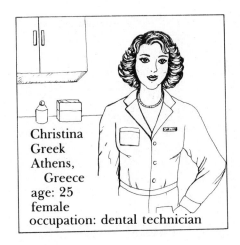

Christina
Greek
Athens,
   Greece
age: 25
female
occupation: dental technician

Avi
Israeli
Tel Aviv,
   Israel
age: 19
male
occupation: undergraduate
   student

Consuelo
Mexican
Vera Cruz,
   Mexico
age: 30
female
occupation: nurse

Anna
Russian
Kiev, Soviet
    Union
age: 32
female
occupation: medical doctor

Michel
French
Marseille,
    France
age: 37
male
occupation: meat packer

Keiko
Japanese
Kyoto, Japan
age: 19
female
occupation:
    high school student

Bjørn
Swedish
Gøteborg,
    Sweden
age: 19
male
occupation: mechanic,
    part-time ski instructor

Hans-Dieter
German
Munich,
    Germany
age: 28
male
occupation:
    English teacher

Hassan
Egyptian
Alexandria,
    Egypt
age: 34
male
occupation: electrical
    engineering student

ADJECTIVES OF NATIONALITY

Meg's grandparents are from Germany. She's a second-generation American.
Darlene's father's family is French, but her mother's family is Lithuanian.
Bill's grandfather is Polish.
His grandmother is Dutch.
Chrissy's teacher is Chinese-American.

Notes

A. The formation of the adjectives of nationality is very irregular.
B. Some general patterns are evident but spelling changes cannot be predicted.

-n or -ian

NATION	NATIONALITY
Australia	Australian
Austria	Austrian
Canada	Canadian
Cuba	Cuban
Egypt	Egyptian
Germany	German
India	Indian
Indonesia	Indonesian
Iran	Iranian / Persian
Italy	Italian
Korea	Korean
Mexico	Mexican
Russia	Russian
USA	American
Venezuela	Venezuelan

-sh

NATION	NATIONALITY
Denmark	Danish
England	English
Finland	Finnish
Ireland	Irish
Poland	Polish
Spain	Spanish
Sweden	Swedish
Turkey	Turkish

-i

NATION	NATIONALITY
Iraq	Iraqi
Israel	Israeli
Saudi Arabia	Saudi

-ese

NATION	NATIONALITY
Burma	Burmese
China	Chinese
Japan	Japanese
Lebanon	Lebanese
Portugal	Portuguese
Taiwan	Taiwanese
Viet Nam	Vietnamese

Other

NATION	NATIONALITY
France	French
Greece	Greek
Holland	Dutch
Soviet Union	Soviet
Switzerland	Swiss
Thailand	Thai

PERSONAL QUESTIONS

NAME	AGE	SEX	OCCUPATION	NATIONALITY	NATIVE COUNTRY	PLACE OF BIRTH
Reza	34	male	electrical engineering student	{Persian Iranian}	Iran	Shiraz
Michel	37	male	meat packer	French	France	Marseille
Keiko	19	female	high school student	Japanese	Japan	Kyoto

INFORMATION QUESTIONS

Questions	Answers	Questions	Answers
Fred	**Reza**	**Fred**	**Reza**
What's your name?	Reza.	What's his name?	His name is Michel.
How old are you?	I'm 34 years old.	How old is he?	He's 37 years old.
What do you do?	I'm a student.	What does he do?	He's a meat packer.
What's your major?	Electrical engineering.	What's his nationality?	He's French.
What's your nationality?	I'm Persian.	Where is he from?	He's from Nice.
Where are you from?	I'm from Teheran.	Where was he born?	Marseille.
Where were you born?	Shiraz.		

Notes

A. Interrogative words WHERE, WHAT, and HOW OLD
   1. WHERE asks about location. (See Chapter Seven.)

   examples   *Where* are you from?
           I'm from *Shiraz.*
                (location)
         Where were you born?
         Santiago, Chile.
         (location)

   2. WHAT sometimes asks about things. (See Chapter Two.)

   examples   *What*'s your major?
           Electrical engineering.
       What's your nationality?
           I'm French.

3. HOW OLD asks about age.

> **examples** *How old* is Michel?
> He's 37.
> (age)
> *How old* are you?
> I'm 19.
> (age)

B. Position: In information questions, WHERE, WHAT, and HOW OLD come at the beginning of the sentence.

1. Questions with the verb BE: Notice the similarity with YES/NO-question word order.

> **examples**
>
> Where {Are you from Tokyo? / are you from?
>
> What {Is his major history? / is his major?
>
> How old {Is she 30 years old? / is she?

2. Questions with other verbs

$$\begin{Bmatrix} \text{WHERE} \\ \text{WHAT} \end{Bmatrix} + \begin{Bmatrix} \text{DOES} \\ \text{DO} \end{Bmatrix} + \underline{\hspace{2cm}} + \underline{\hspace{2cm}}$$
(subject) (base form of the verb)

a. DOES is used before the third person singular subject.

> **examples** Where does Jonathan study?   What does Chrissy eat for dinner?
> At the library.   A hamburger and French fries.

b. DO is used before all other subjects.

> **examples** Where do your parents live?   What do you do?
> In Chicago.   I'm a meat packer.

C. Responses to personal questions

1. Long answers

INTERROGATIVE	QUESTION	LONG RESPONSE
WHERE	*Where* are you from?	I am from *Iran*.
WHAT	*What* is your major?	My major is *engineering*.
HOW OLD	*How old* are you?	I am *34 years old*.

2. Short answers: These are common in spoken English.

INTERROGATIVE	QUESTION	SHORT RESPONSE
WHERE	*Where* do your parents live?	*Guadalajara*.
WHAT	*What* is your name?	*Anna*.
HOW OLD	*How old* is Michel?	*37*.

3. Other common answers

> **examples** {What do you do? / What is your occupation?} I'm a teacher.
>
> What is your nationality?   I'm American.

EXERCISE #1. PARTS OF THE BODY. LEVEL A.

Directions Fill in the blanks on the photos below with the names of the parts of the body.

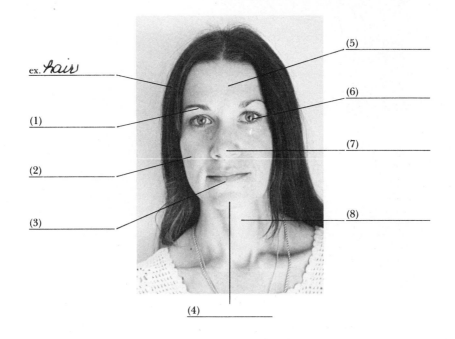

ex. *hair*

(1) _____

(2) _____

(3) _____

(5) _____

(6) _____

(7) _____

(8) _____

(4) _____

(2) _____

(1) _____

(3) _____

(4) _____

(5) _____

(6) _____

(7) _____

(9) _____

(11) _____

(8) _____

(10) _____

(12) _____

Name: _____ Date: _____ **123**

EXERCISE #2. COMPARISONS. LEVEL A.

Directions Fill in the blanks with the correct form of the comparative.

      example   *Susie:*   Hi, Darlene.
                     Darlene: Hi.
                     Susie: You're home _**earlier**_ today than yesterday.
                                                      EARLY

Darlene: Yeah. I'm really tired. It's so hot today.

Susie: Yeah, it's _____ than yesterday, and it's _____ too.
                        (1) HOT   (2) SMOGGY

Darlene: And the traffic is horrible!

Susie: Well, it's Friday. The traffic is always _____ on Friday.
                                                 (3) BAD

Darlene: Let's have something to drink. I'm thirsty.

Susie: I have some leftover coffee on the stove.

Darlene: It's so hot today . . . what about something cold?

Susie: Let's make iced coffee.

Darlene: That's _____.
                  (4) GOOD

Susie: So, let's hear about your day. How are the apartments in Santa Monica?

Darlene: They're _____ than the apartments in Venice, but they're also
                             (5) NICE

_____.
(6) EXPENSIVE.

Susie: That's true, but Santa Monica is _____, and the area is _____.
                                       (7) SAFE   (8) BEAUTIFUL

Darlene: I know, but I'm not earning enough. Besides, most of the apartment buildings in Santa Monica are _____. and the apartments are usually _____ in new buildings.
(9) NEW   (10) SMALL

Susie: Are the apartments in Venice _____?
(11) LARGE

Darlene: Yeah, most of the buildings are _____, and they usually have _____ rooms.
(12) OLD   (13) BIG

Susie: But the neighborhood is so run-down! Santa Monica is much _____.
(14) PRETTY

Darlene: It's pretty, but Venice has a lot of charm. It's close to the beach, and there are lots of cute shops and restaurants . . . and the old buildings are so interesting!

Susie: It *is* a _____ neighborhood than Santa Monica, but I still like Santa Monica.
(15) INTERESTING

Darlene: Well, I'm still looking in both places. Maybe there are cheap apartments somewhere in Santa Monica.

Susie: Let's hope so.

EXERCISE #3. *HAVE/BE.* LEVEL A.

Directions Fill in the blank with the correct form of HAVE or BE.

example Chrissy's hair *is*n't curly. She *has* straight hair.

1. Chrissy _____ short, but she _____ long legs. Her hair _____ long,
(1)   (2)   (3)

and she _____ blue eyes. She _____ freckles, and her nose _____ cute. She
(4)   (5)   (6)

_____ very thin. Her complexion _____ clear, and she _____ fair skin.
(7)   (8)   (9)

Name: _____   Date: _____

2.   Meg _____ average in size, but Gary _____ tall and thin. They _____
                   (1)   (2)   (3)

athletic. Gary _____ straight hair, but Meg's hair _____ curly. Meg _____ dark
                   (4)   (5)   (6)

hair, but Gary's hair _____ light. Gary _____ 20–20 vision. His eyes _____ per-
                      (7)   (8)   (9)

fect. Gary _____ a beard and a moustache.
            (10)

EXERCISE #4. REVIEW. LEVEL A.

Directions Complete the description of the person using the personal data on pages 118 and 119.

      example I am 25 years old. I'm a dental technician.
                My name is ___*Christina*___ and I'm ___*Greek*___ .

1. I'm American. I'm from _____. I'm 26 years old and I have a job as a _____.

2. I'm 22 years old. I'm an electrical engineering student. I'm _____ and I'm from Shiraz.
   My name is _____.

3. I'm a nurse and I'm from _____. _____ _____ is Consuelo and
   _____ 30 years old.

4. I'm 16 years old and I'm a _____. I'm _____ and I'm from _____.
   My name is _____.

5. I'm a _____ and I'm 19. I'm _____ and I'm from Tel Aviv. My
   _____ _____ Avi.

6. I'm _____ _____, France. I'm a _____ _____.

_____ 37 _____ _____. _____ _____

_____Michel.

7. I'm _____ _____ teacher. I'm _____ and I'm _____

_____, Germany. _____ 28 _____ _____.

My _____ -_____.

8. _____19 _____ _____. _____ a _____

and a _____-_____ _____ _____. I'm

_____ and I'm from _____, _____. My name is

_____.

EXERCISE #5.   COMPARISONS.   PART I.   LEVEL B.

Directions   Look at the following pictures. Then, using the words given, write two sentences for each picture with HAVE or BE.

    a. Write one sentence with the base form of the adjective.

    b. Write one sentence with the comparative form of the adjective.

example a. *Meg has curly hair.*

           b. *Meg has curlier hair than Darlene.*

1.

dark hair

a. _____.

b. _____.

2.

short

a. _____.

b. _____.

Name: _____   Date: _____

3.

thin

a. _____ .

b. _____ .

4.

athletic

a. _____ .

b. _____ .

5.

serious

a. _____ .

b. _____ .

EXERCISE #5. COMPARISONS. PART II. LEVEL B.

Directions Look at the following pictures. Then, using the words given, write two sentences for each picture. Use the comparative form.

example straight hair / curly hair

a. *Darlene's hair is straighter than Meg's* .

b. *Meg's hair is curlier than Darlene's* .

1.

young /old
a. _____ .
b. _____ .

2.

good vision / bad vision
a. _____ .
b. _____ .

3.

heavy / light
a. _____ .
b. _____ .

4.
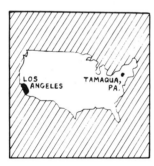
big / small
a. _____ .
b. _____ .

5.
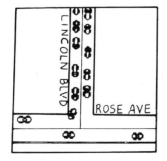
busy / quiet
a. _____ .
b. _____ .

Name: _____ Date: _____

EXERCISE #6. *HAVE/BE.* LEVEL B.

Directions   Write sentences with the information given. Write one sentence with HAVE and one sentence with BE when possible.

examples   CHRISSY

long hair   a. *Chrissy has long hair*.
            b. *Her hair is long*   .
freckles   a. *She has freckles*   .

Darlene

1. long dark hair

     a. _____

     b. _____
2. green eyes

     a. _____

     b. _____
3. tall and thin

     a. _____
4. straight teeth

     a. _____

     b. _____
5. small eyes

     a. _____

     b. _____
6. pretty

     a. _____

Gary

1. tall and thin

   a. _____

2. moustache and beard

   a. _____

3. wavy hair

   a. _____

   b. _____

4. crooked teeth

   a. _____

   b. _____

5. big feet

   a. _____

   b. _____

EXERCISE #7.   ANSWERING PERSONAL QUESTIONS.   LEVEL B.

Directions   Refer to pages 118 and 119. Answer the questions with a complete sentence.

examples   1. What is her name?

Her name is Anna.

2. Where is she from?

She's from Kiev.

Anna

1. **Anna**

   a. What is Anna's nationality?

   _____

   b. How old is she?

   _____

   c. What does she do?

   _____

2. **Michel**

   a. How old is Michel?

   _____

   b. Where is he from?

   _____

   c. What is his nationality?

   _____

Name: _____   Date: _____

3.

Consuelo

a. What does she do?

_____

b. Where is she from?

_____

c. What's her nationality?

_____

4.

Hans-Dieter

a. What's his name?

_____

b. What does he do?

_____

c. How old is he?

_____

5.

You

a. What's your name?

_____

b. How old are you?

_____

c. Where are you from?

_____

d. What's your nationality?

_____

e. What do you do?

_____

EXERCISE #8.   ASKING PERSONAL QUESTIONS.   LEVEL B.

Directions   a. Ask an information question about the information given under the picture.
b. Then write a sentence answering the question.

Anna

example

a. *How old is she ?*

b. *She's 32 years old.*

32 years old

1.   Reza

Persian

a. _____

b. _____

2.   Michel

Meat packer

a. _____

b. _____

3.   Hassan

Hassan

a. _____

b. _____

4.   Bjørn

Mechanic, part-time ski instructor

a. _____

b. _____

5.   Keiko

19 years old

a. _____

b. _____

6.   Christina

Athens, Greece

a. _____

b. _____

7.   Avi

Israeli

a. _____

b. _____

8.   Elizabeth

Elizabeth

a. _____

b. _____

Name: _____   Date: _____

9. Fred

Kansas City,
Kansas

a. _____
b. _____

10. Hans-
Dieter

28 years old

a. _____
b. _____

EXERCISE #9. PART I. LEVEL C.

Directions Look at page 118 and page 119 for information about the people below.
1. Read the dialogue between Hans-Dieter and Hassan.
2. Write a dialogue between Keiko and Bjørn, and between Elizabeth and Christina.

Hans-Dieter

Hi. I'm Hans-Dieter. What's your name?

I'm from Munich, Germany. What do you do?

I'm an English teacher.

Hassan

My name is Hassan. I'm from Egypt. Where are you from?

I'm an electrical engineering student. What's your occupation?

Keiko

Bjorn

_____
_____
_____
_____
_____
_____

_____
_____
_____
_____
_____
_____

Elizabeth

Christina

_____

_____

_____

_____

_____

_____

_____

_____

_____

_____

_____

_____

_____

_____

_____

_____

_____

_____

EXERCISE #9. PART II. LEVEL C.

Directions Write a dialogue between you and one of your classmates using similar information.

You

_____
(your classmate)

_____

_____

_____

_____

_____

_____

_____

_____

_____

_____

_____

_____

_____

_____

_____

_____

_____

_____

_____

_____

_____

_____

_____

_____

_____

_____

Name: _____   Date: _____

EXERCISE #10. PART I. LEVEL C.

Directions   1. Read the model paragraph below.
2. Write a paragraph describing Meg's father.
3. Write a paragraph describing Jonathan's sister.

Bill's mother

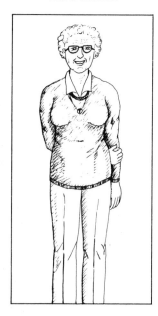

Model paragraph

Bill's mother is 52 years old. She has short, blond, curly hair. Her eyes are blue. She's near-sighted and has glasses. She has a nice smile, and her teeth are straight. She's short and plump.

Meg's father

Jonathan's sister

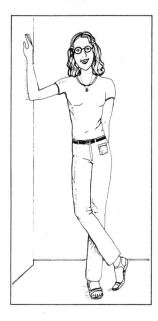

_____

_____

_____

_____

_____

_____

_____

_____

_____

_____

EXERCISE #10.   PART II.   LEVEL C.

Directions   1. Draw a picture of a friend or of your teacher.
                2. Write a paragraph describing him or her.

_____

_____

_____

_____

_____

_____

_____

_____

_____

_____

Name: _____   Date: _____   **137**

EXERCISE #10.   PART III.   LEVEL C.

Directions   1. Draw your self-portrait.
2. Write a paragraph describing yourself.

LOOKING FOR
AN APARTMENT

At Jonathan and Gary's apartment

Bill: Where's today's newspaper?

Jonathan: Over there, on the coffee table.

Bill: Let's look at the classified section. Is there anything to drink? I need a beer.

Jonathan: Beer!? It's only 10 o'clock in the morning.

Bill: Why not? I like beer. What's wrong with that?
(The doorbell rings.)

Gary: There's the doorbell.

Darlene: We're here! Sorry we're late. This place is hard to find because there are no numbers on these apartment buildings.

Gary: That's okay. You're only five minutes late.

Darlene: Oh, this is our friend, Meg.

Jonathan, Gary, and Bill: Hi.

Meg: Hi.

Bill: And I'm Bill, Jon and Gary's ex-neighbor.

Meg: I really like your apartment.

Gary: Yeah, we like it too.

Meg:	Why are you moving, then?
Gary:	Because the rent here is too high.
Meg:	Is it a two-bedroom?
Jonathan:	No, there's only one bedroom, and it's really tiny.
Bill:	Here's an apartment in the classified section of the paper. It has four bedrooms. It's in the Marina, and it's only $800 a month.
Meg:	I love the Marina.
Bill:	I like it too. I'm living there now. I'm only moving because my rent is too high.
Meg:	Where's your apartment?
Bill:	On Villa Marina Way, near Donkin's Bar.
Meg:	Those apartments are really nice. They have swimming pools and saunas, and all the apartments have balconies.
Jonathan:	The Marina is too expensive.
Gary:	And too "plastic."
Meg:	It *isn't* plastic. It's modern, and the rent is high because it's a nice location.
Gary:	Darlene . . . what about the house in Venice?
Darlene:	Oh, I have bad news. It's not for rent.
Gary:	Why isn't it for rent? Aren't your friends moving?
Darlene:	Yes, they are, but the owner is selling the house.
Gary:	Oh, that's too bad.
Jonathan:	Here's a house in Venice. It has five bedrooms and a yard. It's only $800 a month.
Darlene:	Where is it?
Jonathan:	It's on Washington Blvd.
Meg:	Oh, that isn't a nice neighborhood.
Darlene:	Why isn't it? What's the neighborhood like there?
Meg:	The houses are really old and run-down. The neighborhood isn't safe. Here's a five-bedroom house in Santa Monica. It's $950 a month. Is that too expensive?
Gary:	Yes, it is.
Bill:	No, it isn't.
Meg:	But it has *five* bedrooms, two and a half bathrooms, a large yard, *and* it's near the beach.
Darlene:	Is the neighborhood there nice? What's it like?
Meg:	The houses are old, but in good condition. There are lots of stores, and the schools are good.
Bill:	Let's look at it.

WANT/NEED/LIKE: SIMPLE PRESENT TENSE STATEMENTS

3rd PERSON SINGULAR FORM (HE/SHE/IT FORM)	OTHER FORMS
Chrissy wants a Coke. Jonathan wants a new motorcycle.	We want a cheap place. I want a house in Venice.
Darlene needs a part-time job. My car needs a tune-up.	We need a five-bedroom house. Meg and Darlene need more exercise.
Gary likes old houses. Bill likes beautiful women.	You like the old houses in Venice. Chrissy and Darlene like the beach.

Notes

A. Form
1. The third person singular form of the verbs, WANT, NEED, and LIKE is the base form of the verb plus -S.

   examples   Chrissy like*s* her elementary school.
   Gary need*s* a haircut.
   Meg want*s* a rich husband.

2. The base form of the verbs is used for other persons.

   examples   Gary and I like old neighborhoods.
   We want quiet neighbors.
   You need a new car.

B. Use
1. The verbs WANT, NEED, and LIKE always take an object.

   examples   Bill likes *beer.*
   (object)
   I need *a vacation.*
   (object)
   Meg wants *an apartment with a sauna.*
   (object)

2. We usually do not use the verbs WANT, NEED, and LIKE in the present progressive form.

DEMONSTRATIVE PRONOUNS AND ADJECTIVES: *THIS/THESE, THAT/THOSE*

This place is hard to find because there are no numbers on these apartment buildings.
Those apartments on Villa Marina Way are really nice.
Is that too expensive?
These are my friends, Darlene and Chrissy.
This is a tiny, one-bedroom apartment.

Notes

A. Form
1. THESE is the plural form of THIS. (See Chapter Two.)

   examples   This apartment is tiny.
   These apartments are too expensive.

2. THOSE is the plural form of THAT. (See Chapter Two.)

   examples   That street is too busy.
   Those apartments in the Marina are really nice.

3. THIS, THAT, THESE, and THOSE can be adjectives. They come before nouns.

   examples   *That neighborhood* is run down.
   (adj.)   (noun)
   Those places all have saunas and balconies.
   (adj.)(noun)

4. THIS, THAT, THESE, and THOSE can be pronouns. They take the place of nouns.

   examples   These are my friends, Darlene and Chrissy.
   What's wrong with that?

B. Use
1. Use THIS and THESE for objects and people near the speaker.

2. Use THAT and THOSE for objects and people far from the speaker.

3. Use THIS, THAT, THESE, and THOSE the first time you point to objects or people. Use the simple subject pronoun for any future references.

   examples   *Those* are beautiful apartments, but *they*'re expensive.
   These apartments here in Westwood are really expensive, and *they*'re too small.

C. Questions with THIS, THAT, THESE, and THOSE:
1. Demonstrative adjectives: In response to a question, the subject pronoun agrees with the modified noun.

   examples   Is *that woman* your friend?
   Yes, *she* is.
   Is *that house* too expensive?
   Yes, *it* is.

2. Demonstrative pronouns: In response to a question, use either IT or THEY.

   examples   Isn't *that* your friend Meg? Yes, *it* is.
   Isn't *this* a nice neighborhood? Yes, *it* is.
   Aren't *those* nice apartments? Yes, *they* are.

WHY + BE

Why are you moving?
   Because the rent is too high.
Why isn't it for rent?
   It's not for rent because the owner is selling the house.
Why isn't it a nice neighborhood?
   The houses are old and run-down.

Notes

A. The interrogative WHY usually asks for a reason.

examples   Why are you moving?
Because the rent here is too high.
(reason)
Why are you late?
I'm late *because the traffic is really heavy today.*
(reason)

1. The interrogative WHY NOT? asks for a reason after a negative statement.

   examples   I'm not going to the beach today.
Why not?
Because it's too hot.

Chrissy isn't eating dinner.
Why not?
She's not hungry.

   a. You can also use WHY NOT? to agree with someone or to accept an invitation.

      examples   Let's go to a movie.
Sure, why not? That's a good idea.
I'm going shopping. Are you coming?
Sure, why not?

B. Position: In information questions WHY comes at the beginning of the sentence. Notice the similarity with YES/NO question word order.

   examples
Why Isn't Bill drinking milk?
Why isn't Bill drinking milk?

Why Are Jonathan and Gary moving?
Why are Jonathan and Gary moving?

C. Responses: The answer to a question with WHY usually gives a reason.
1. Long answers: The long response to a WHY question usually includes a BECAUSE clause.

   examples   Why are you eating now?
I'm eating *because I'm hungry.*
Why is Bill drinking beer at 10 o'clock in the morning?
He's drinking beer *because he likes beer.*

2. Short answers: These are common in spoken English.
   a. Short answers frequently begin with BECAUSE.

      examples   Why aren't you looking in Westwood?
Because the apartments there are too expensive.
Why aren't you staying in Pasadena?
Because it's too far from the university.

   b. You can omit BECAUSE from the answer.

      examples   Why isn't it a nice neighborhood?
(Because) the houses are old and run-down.
Why are you home early?
(Because) I'm going grocery shopping before dinner.

BECAUSE

Darlene and Chrissy like Santa Monica because it's a safe neighborhood.
Jonathan and Gary want a house in Venice because there are nice old houses there.
Those apartments are really nice because they have swimming pools and saunas.

Notes

A. BECAUSE introduces a statement which gives a cause or reason.

B. BECAUSE can join two sentences. When a noun is repeated in the second sentence, you can use a pronoun or a phrase indicating location in place of the repeated noun.

> **example**   statement: *Chrissy* wants a Coke.
>   reason: *Chrissy* is thirsty.
>
>   ⎣⟶ Chrissy wants a Coke *because she* is thirsty.
>
>   statement: Darlene likes *Santa Monica.*
>   reason: The schools are good in *Santa Monica.*
>
>   ⎣⟶ Darlene likes Santa Monica *because* the schools are good (there).

C. Position: The BECAUSE clause can come at the beginning or end of a sentence. When it comes at the beginning of the sentence, use a comma after the BECAUSE clause.

> **examples**   statement: They need a large apartment or a house.
>   reason: There are five people.
>
>   ⮡ They need a large apartment or a house *because there are five people.*
>
>   ⮡ *Because there are five people,* they need a large apartment or a house.

EXPLETIVE *IT*

> It's six o'clock.
> It's raining today.
> It's only two blocks to the market.
> Who's that? It's the landlord, Mr. Garvey.

Notes

A. Use the pronoun IT to introduce the following ideas:
  1. Time

> **examples** It's six o'clock.
>   It's seven-thirty.

  2. Weather conditions

> **examples** It's raining today.
>   It's frequently cold and foggy near the beach.

  3. Distance

> **examples** It's only two blocks to the market.
>   It's five miles to campus from Venice.

  4. Identification

> **examples** Who's that?
>   It's the landlord, Mr. Garvey.
>   Who's at the door?
>   Oh, it's one of Bill's girlfriends.

TIME: WHAT TIME IS IT?

It's six o'clock.
Darlene is getting up.

It's $\begin{cases}\text{half past six.}\\\text{six-thirty.}\end{cases}$

Chrissy is getting up. Darlene is making breakfast for Chrissy.

It's $\begin{cases}\text{six forty-five.}\\\text{a quarter to seven.}\end{cases}$

Chrissy is getting dressed and ready for school.

It's $\begin{cases}\text{five to seven.}\\\text{six fifty-five.}\end{cases}$

Breakfast is ready.

It's seven o'clock, and Chrissy is eating breakfast.

It's $\begin{cases}\text{seven ten.}\\\text{ten after seven.}\end{cases}$

Chrissy is brushing her teeth.

It's $\begin{cases}\text{seven twenty-five.}\\\text{twenty-five after seven.}\end{cases}$

Chrissy and her friend are leaving for school.

NUMBER-NOUN COMBINATIONS

The apartment is in an old two-story building.
This apartment has three bedrooms and one-and-a-half baths.
Bill has an 8-track stereo in his car.
Chrissy wants a new 10-speed bike.
Darlene's car has two doors.

Notes

A. Form
  1. Noun form: Use the plural noun form after a number greater than one.

     examples Large Cokes are 50 cents.
                   The temperature is 80 degrees.

  2. Adjective form: A number-noun combination before another noun functions as an adjective. The noun after the number is not plural.
     a. Use a hyphen (-) between the number and the noun.

        examples Chrissy has a 3-speed bike.
                      We need a two-car garage.

NOUN FORM	ADJECTIVE FORM
The house has five bedrooms.	It's a five-bedroom house.
My car has two doors.	It's a two-door car.
Those buildings have two stories.	They are two-story buildings.

HERE/THERE

The apartments here in Westwood are too expensive.
Here's an ad for an apartment in the Marina.
What's the neighborhood like there?
The neighborhood there isn't safe.

Notes

A. Meaning
  1. Use HERE to talk about a location near the speaker.

     examples The apartments here in Westwood are too expensive.
                   The climate here is hot and dry.

  2. Use THERE to talk about a location far from the speaker.

     examples Our apartment is there across the street.
                   The bus stop is over there by the drug store.

B. When they refer to location, HERE and THERE are usually stressed in speech.

   examples Your glasses are hére on the table.
                 The gas station is thére on the corner.

  1. Don't confuse the stressed THERE of location with the unstressed expletive THERE. (See Chapter Three.)

     examples There's a gás station on the corner. (expletive THERE)
                   Thére's the gás station on the corner. (expression of location)

C. Position
1. HERE and THERE can come at the beginning of a sentence.

examples *Here* are your glasses. They're on the table.
There's Meg. She's at the end of the line.

2. HERE and THERE can come after a verb.

examples She's *waiting there* in the cafeteria.
(verb)
My *car's here*.
(verb).

3. HERE and THERE can come after a noun.

examples The *apartments there* are too expensive.
(noun)
I like the mild *climate here*.
(noun)

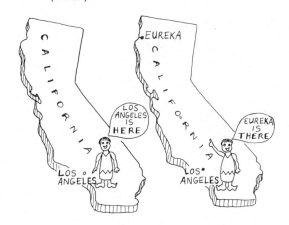

ADJECTIVES: ADDITIONAL VOCABULARY

NEIGHBORHOODS	STREETS	TRAFFIC
old/modern	busy	heavy/light
run-down/well-kept	congested	noisy
suburban/inner-city	safe/unsafe	congested
business/residential	quiet/noisy	bumper-to-bumper

WEATHER	AIR QUALITY	HOUSES
humid/dry	smoggy/clean	old/modern
clear/cloudy	polluted	run-down/well-kept
foggy		dingy/pleasant
hazy		stuffy/airy
sunny/rainy		

EXERCISE #1. THE SIMPLE PRESENT TENSE. LEVEL A.

Directions   Write the correct form of the given verb in the blanks.

example   Chrissy _____*wants*_____ a Coke.
                            WANT

At the cafeteria

Darlene: Let's find a table.

Chrissy: There _____ a free table, over there.
                          (1) BE

Darlene: But there _____n't any chairs at that table. Let's sit there in the corner. That table
                                (2) BE

            _____ free.
                (3) BE

Chrissy: Okay.

Darlene: It _____ so hot outside. I _____ something cold to drink.
                    (4) BE   (5) NEED

Chrissy: Me too. I _____ a Coke.
                        (6) WANT

Darlene: Let's get some milk for you. Soft drinks _____ bad for your teeth.
                                                        (7) BE

Chrissy: But I _____ Coke. All kids _____ Coke.
                    (8) LIKE   (9) LIKE

Darlene: Yes, but you _____ vitamins. There _____n't any vitamins in Coke.
                            (10) NEED   (11) BE

Chrissy: Okay, but I _____ a hamburger and fries. Hamburgers _____ lots of vita-
                          (12) WANT   (13) HAVE
            mins.

Name: _____   Date: _____   **149**

Darlene: Hamburgers _____ too greasy . . . what about a salad? Salads _____

                (14) BE   (15) HAVE

          vitamins.

Chrissy: But I _____ hamburgers. Jonathan _____ hamburgers too, and he

                  (16) LIKE   (17) LIKE

          _____ healthy.

                (18) BE

Darlene: That _____ not a good argument. Jonathan _____ terrible eating habits.

                  (19) BE   (20) HAVE

          Anyway, a growing child _____ good food.

                                (21) NEED

Chrissy: But I _____ a hamburger

                (22) WANT

Darlene: Okay, . . . a hamburger, but no fries, . . . and milk, not Coke.

Chrissy: Okay, it's a deal.

EXERCISE #2. DEMONSTRATIVES. LEVEL A.

Directions Fill in the blank with THIS, THAT, THESE, or THOSE.

    example ___*These*___ apartments here in Westwood are too expensive.

Chrissy: _____ is a great apartment, Jonathan.

                (1)

Jonathan: Thanks, Chrissy. We like it, too.

Chrissy: I like the balcony here. Are there balconies in all _____ apartments?

                                                                  (2)

Jonathan: No, we're paying extra for it.

Chrissy: Is there a swimming pool here?

Jonathan: Not in _____ building, but there's a pool in _____ building **across the**
                                    (3)   (4)

street. It's a really fancy building. All _____ apartments have fireplaces and balconies,
                                                        (5)
and there are saunas.

Chrissy: Oh, great! Let's get an apartment in the building across the street with a fireplace, **a balcony,**
and a sauna.

Darlene: Let's be realistic. _____ apartments are too expensive. We need a low-**rent neighbor-**
                                        (6)

hood. Anyway, I like old places. Modern apartments like _____ **here in Westwood**
                                                                        (7)
are too "plastic."

Jonathan: Venice is a low-rent area, and it's near the beach!

Darlene: Isn't _____ a really run-down neighborhood?
                        (8)

Jonathan: Not really. The buildings are old, but not run-down. There are **some listings in today's paper**
for houses in Venice.

Darlene: Is _____ today's paper, over there in the corner?
                        (9)

Jonathan: Yeah, it is.

Darlene: Let's look at it.

Chrissy: _____'s a good idea.
                    (10)

EXERCISE #3.   INTERROGATIVES.   LEVEL A.

Directions   Fill in the blank with WHO / WHOSE / WHAT / WHY / HOW OLD.

    example   *Mr. Garvey:*   ____*Why*____ are you looking for a place in Venice?
               Gary: Because we like the beach.

Name: _____   Date: _____

Mr. Garvey:	Hello.
Jonathan and Gary:	Hi.
Gary:	Are you Mr. Garvey?
Mr. Garvey:	Yes, I am.
Gary:	There's an ad in the paper today for a five-bedroom house. Is the house still for rent?
Mr. Garvey:	Yes, it is.
Jonathan and Gary:	Great!
Gary:	A five-bedroom house is perfect.
Mr. Garvey:	_____ are you looking for a large house? (1)
Jonathan:	Well, we have four friends. . .
Mr. Garvey:	Friends? _____ do your friends do? (2)
Jonathan:	Darlene and Meg are students at the university, and Bill is a tennis teacher.
Mr. Garvey:	Hmm . . . and _____ do you do? (3)
Jonathan:	I'm a student, and Gary is a third-grade teacher.
Mr. Garvey:	Well, that's okay. Let's go look at the house.
Gary:	This is a nice old neighborhood.
Mr. Garvey:	Yes, my wife and I like it here. It isn't very smoggy, and the beach is only 3½ blocks away.
Gary:	This is a great house. _____ is it? (4)
Mr. Garvey:	I think it's about 40 years old. It has nice high ceilings and large rooms.
Gary and Jonathan:	Fantastic!
Gary:	I really like these rooms.
Jonathan:	_____ furniture is that? (5)
Mr. Garvey:	That's the Browns' furniture. They're still moving out.
Gary:	_____ are they moving? (6)
Mr. Garvey:	Mr. Brown has a new job in Albany, New York.
Gary:	Oh.
Mr. Garvey:	There's a beautiful, big back yard.
Jonathan:	It's really nice. _____'s that man next to the garage? (7)
Mr. Garvey:	That's Mr. Bradley. He's helping with the painting.
Gary:	Are there any children on this block?
Mr. Garvey:	Yes, the neighbors have twins.
Jonathan:	_____ are they? (8)
Mr. Garvey:	I think they're about six. _____ are you asking? (9)

Gary:	Because Darlene has a daughter.
Mr. Garvey:	_____ is her daughter?
	(10)
Gary:	She's seven.
Mr. Garvey:	_____ 's her name?
	(11)
Jonathan:	Chrissy.
Mr. Garvey:	Is she well-behaved?
Gary:	Oh, yes. She's very quiet.
Jonathan:	She's no trouble at all.
Mr. Garvey:	Hmm. _____ 's signing the lease?
	(12)
Gary:	I am.
Mr. Garvey:	Well, are you interested in the house?
Jonathan:	Yeah.
Gary:	Definitely. We're meeting our friends later this afternoon.
Mr. Garvey:	Okay. Here's my telephone number. Let me know soon.
Gary:	Okay. Sure.
Jonathan:	Thanks, Mr. Garvey.
Mr. Garvey:	Good bye.

EXERCISE #4. *BECAUSE.* LEVEL A.

Directions   Combine the two sentences with BECAUSE. Use a pronoun in the second part of the sentence when possible.

examples   1. I don't like the Marina.
The Marina is too "plastic."

I don't like the Marina because it's too "plastic."

2. Chrissy is hungry.
Chrissy is eating a hamburger.

Chrissy is eating a hamburger because she's hungry.

1. Bill is reading the newspaper.
Bill is looking for an apartment.

_____

_____

2. Santa Monica has good schools.
Darlene and Chrissy like Santa Monica.

_____

_____

3. We like the beach.
We want an apartment in Santa Monica.

_____

_____

Name: _____   Date: _____

4. Those apartments are expensive.
   Those apartments all have saunas and balconies.

   _____

   _____

5. That house isn't large enough.
   That house only has two bedrooms.

   _____

   _____

6. The apartments in Westwood are near the university.
   The apartments in Westwood are expensive.

   _____

   _____

7. Gary and Jonathan like the old houses in Venice.
   Gary and Jonathan want a house in Venice.

   _____

   _____

8. Meg wants a place near the university.
   Meg is a student.

   _____

   _____

9. Bill likes beer.
   Bill wants a beer at 10 o'clock in the morning.

   _____

   _____

10. Darlene has a date tonight.
    Darlene needs a babysitter.

    _____

    _____

EXERCISE #5. TIME. LEVEL A.

Directions   Write a sentence giving the correct time. Write out the words for the time.

example   *It's five o'clock.*
Gary is making dinner.

1.

_____
Jonathan is studying.

2.

Dinner is ready.

_____

3.

Jonathan and Gary are finishing dinner.
Gary is hurrying because he has a date with
Adrienne tonight.

_____

4.

The telephone is ringing. It's Adrienne.

_____

5.

_____and
Gary is taking a shower.

6.

The telephone is ringing again. It's Darlene.

_____

7.

Gary is leaving.

_____

8.

Gary's arriving at Adrienne's apartment.

He's late. _____

Name: _____   Date: _____

EXERCISE #6. *HERE/THERE.* LEVEL A.

Directions   Fill in the blank with HERE or THERE.

   example   *Adrienne:*   Let's spend the evening ___*here*___ in my apartment.

At Adrienne's apartment in Santa Monica

Gary: Hi. I'm sorry I'm late. The traffic is really heavy tonight.

Adrienne: I'm glad you're finally _____. Your dinner is getting cold.
                                                    (1)

Gary: Are we eating dinner _____?
                                              (2)

Adrienne: Yes, I'm making fried chicken.

Gary: That's great. I'm really tired. Let's spend a quiet evening _____.
                                                                                      (3)

Adrienne: Aren't we going to a movie tonight?

Gary: Oh, let's just watch television . . . where's your guide?

Adrienne: It's over _____ on the coffee table.
                                 (4)

Gary: Hmmm . . . Let's see . . . What about "Planet of the Gorillas?" Adrienne? Where are you?

Adrienne: I'm in _____, in the kitchen. Our dinner is burning.
                              (5)

Gary: There's a good science fiction movie called "Planet of the Gorillas."

Adrienne: Okay, let's watch it. Why are you so tired tonight?

Gary: Oh, this apartment search is taking too long.

Adrienne: Why? What's the problem?

Gary: We all want something different. Jon and I want a place in Venice because we like the old

               houses _____, but Bill and Meg like modern apartments.
                              (6)

Adrienne: There are lots of modern places in the Marina.

Gary: Yeah, they're looking _____, but the rents are too high in that area.
                                             (7)

Adrienne: What about this neighborhood? The rents aren't too high _____.
                                                                            (8)

Gary: Well, Darlene and Chrissy like it _____ because the neighborhood is safe.
                                                      (9)

Adrienne: They're right. The neighborhood _____ is safe, and the houses are nice. The houses
                                                   (10)

in Venice are run-down, and the neighborhood _____ isn't very safe.
                                                    (11)

Gary: But there aren't any cheap houses _____ in Santa Monica.
                                                      (12)

Adrienne: Sure there are. Let's look in today's paper. It's over _____ in the corner.
                                                                        (13)

EXERCISE #7.   *WHY.*   LEVEL B.

Directions   Write a question with WHY in the following dialogue.

      example   *Meg:* ___Why are you so pale___?
                    Darlene: I'm pale because I'm always inside.

Darlene: _____?
                                         (1)

Meg: I'm quiet because I'm somewhat depressed today.

Darlene: Depressed? _____?
                                         (2)

Meg: I'm depressed because I'm having problems with Brian.
Darlene: Brian? Isn't your boyfriend's name Greg?
Meg: Greg's in Europe. I'm going out with Brian while he's away.
Darlene: Poor Greg! He's so naive.

Name: _____   Date: _____

Meg: Naive? Greg? I'm sure he's meeting other women in Europe . . . today an Italian . . . tomorrow a German. . .

Darlene: _____?
(3)

Meg: He's in Europe because he has business there. His company is paying for the trip.

Darlene: _____?
(4)

Meg: They're paying for the trip because it's a training program. He's learning about international management.

Darlene: How long is he staying there?

Meg: Three months.

Darlene: Wow! That's a long training program.

Meg: It's only a six-week program, but he's combining the business trip with a vacation.

Darlene: _____?
(5)

Meg: The program's in Europe because the company's main office is there.

Darlene: That's a fantastic opportunity for Greg.

Meg: Yeah, but it's not so fantastic for me.

Darlene: Tell me more about Brian.

_____?
(6)

Meg: I'm having problems because he's so jealous of Greg.

Darlene: Hmm. That's understandable.

Meg: He's also very egotistical and chauvinistic. He's driving me crazy.

Darlene: _____?
(7)

Meg: I'm going out with him because I'm lonely. Besides, he has money and we always have dinner at expensive restaurants.

Darlene: Meg! That's terrible.

Darlene: _____?
(8)

Darlene: It's terrible because you're using him.

Meg: Maybe you're right.

Darlene: Of course I'm right.

Meg: But Greg isn't coming home for six weeks . . .

Darlene: ?!*?!

EXERCISE #8. *BECAUSE.* LEVEL B.

Directions Complete the following sentences. Use BECAUSE.

examples 1. I want a Coke _because I'm thirsty_.
2. _I'm moving next week because_ my rent is too high.

1. I like this class _____

2. I like my teacher _____

3. I'm studying English _____

4. I $\begin{Bmatrix} \text{like} \\ \text{don't like} \end{Bmatrix}$ my apartment _____

5. _____ I'm hungry.

6. You need lots of **money in the United States** _____

_____

7. _____ the traffic is heavy.

8. I $\begin{Bmatrix} \text{like} \\ \text{don't like} \end{Bmatrix}$ American food _____

_____

9. _____ it's too noisy.

10. I $\begin{Bmatrix} \text{like} \\ \text{don't like} \end{Bmatrix}$ the climate here _____

EXERCISE #9. NUMBER/NOUN COMBINATIONS. LEVEL B.

Directions Write two sentences for each picture.
   a. Use the noun form.
   b. Use the adjective form.

example What's your apartment building like?

a. _It has three stories._

b. _It's a three - story building._

1.

What's the building like?

a. _____

b. _____

2.

What's the car like?

a. _____

b. _____

3.

What's the house like?

a. _____

b. _____

Name: _____   Date: _____

4.

What's the hotel like?

a. _____

b. _____

5.

What's the bike like?

a. _____

b. _____

EXERCISE #10. PART I. LEVEL C.

	JONATHAN AND GARY	MEG	DARLENE AND CHRISSY	BILL
WHAT THEY LIKE	old houses the beach Venice	modern apartments the beach the Marina	old houses the beach Santa Monica	modern apartments the beach the Marina

Directions Look at the chart above. Then read the model paragraph below about what Chrissy, Darlene, Meg, Jonathan, Gary, and Bill like.

Model paragraph

Jonathan, Gary, Meg, Bill, Darlene, and Chrissy are looking for a house or an apartment. Meg and Bill like modern apartments, but Jonathan, Gary, Darlene, and Chrissy like old houses. Jonathan and Gary like Venice because they like the old houses there. Darlene and Chrissy like old houses too, but they like Santa Monica because the neighborhood there is safe. Meg and Bill like the Marina because they like the modern apartments there. They all want a place near the beach because they all like the beach.

EXERCISE #10.   PART II.   LEVEL C.

	JONATHAN AND GARY	MEG	DARLENE AND CHRISSY	BILL
WHAT THEY WANT	a cheap place a yard a fireplace	a cheap place a swimming pool a sauna	a cheap place a safe neighborhood a fireplace	a cheap place a tennis court a balcony

Directions   Look at the chart above. Write a paragraph about what Chrissy, Darlene, Meg, Jonathan, Gary, and Bill want.

Your paragraph

_____

_____

_____

_____

_____

_____

_____

_____

_____

_____

_____

_____

_____

_____

_____

EXERCISE #10. PART III. LEVEL C.

	_____	
	(your name)	
WHAT YOU WANT	_____	_____
	_____	_____
WHAT YOU NEED	_____	_____
	_____	_____

Directions Fill in the chart above with information about the kind of house or apartment you want or need. Then write a paragraph using this information.

_____

_____

_____

_____

_____

_____

_____

_____

_____

_____

_____

_____

_____

_____

_____

_____

_____

_____

EXERCISE #11. LEVEL C.

Directions   Read the model paragraph. Write a paragraph describing your neighborhood. Use the adjectives on page 148.

Model paragraph

My apartment is in Santa Monica on Pico Blvd. The streets in my neighborhood are very busy and noisy because Pico Blvd. is a main business street. The traffic is heavy. The air here is not too polluted because Santa Monica is close to the beach. The air is humid, and sometimes it is hazy and foggy. The apartments in my neighborhood are old and run-down. I like my apartment because the rent is cheap, but the neighborhood is not safe and my apartment is too small and dark.

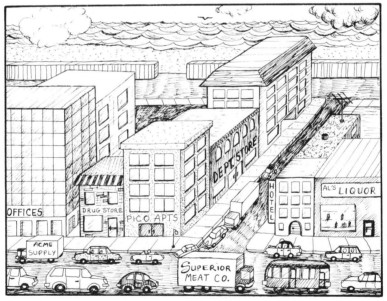

Your neighborhood

_____

_____

_____

_____

_____

Name: _____   Date: _____   **163**

AT
THE PIER

Chrissy: Where are we meeting Gary and Jonathan?

Darlene: Here in Santa Monica at the pier in front of the merry-go-round.

Chrissy: There they are! I can see Gary.

Darlene: Where?

Chrissy: At the hot dog stand. There's Jonathan, too. He's at the front of the line buying a hot dog.

Darlene: Let's walk over there.

Chrissy:	Hi, Jonathan. Hi, Gary.
Jonathan & Gary:	Hi.
Chrissy:	Are the hot dogs good?
Jonathan:	Mmmm . . . hmmm.
Chrissy:	Can I have a hot dog?
Darlene:	No, we're having dinner at 5:00.
Chrissy:	But Jonathan's having a hot dog.
Jonathan:	I'm celebrating.
Darlene:	Celebrating?
Jonathan:	Yeah, we have great news. There's a five-bedroom house in Venice.
Darlene:	Where is it?
Gary:	It's on Rose Avenue near the beach. It's really perfect. There's a yard, and a large garage, and a fireplace in the living room. And the kitchen is large and sunny.
Darlene:	Is the rent high?
Jonathan:	That's the good news. It's only $850 a month plus utilities.
Darlene:	Is there any deposit?
Gary:	No, not really, but we have to pay the last month's rent in advance.
Darlene:	Is it far to the beach?
Gary:	It's about 3½ blocks.
Darlene:	What's the neighborhood like?
Jonathan:	It's nice. There are a lot of old houses on the block, but they're not run-down.
Gary:	Yeah, and there aren't many apartment buildings in the neighborhood.
Darlene:	Is there a lot of traffic on the street?
Gary:	There's not much. The street's very quiet.
Darlene:	Can we look at it today?
Jonathan:	Sure, let's go.

THE MODAL *CAN*

	I	can	meet	you this afternoon.
	Chrissy	can	ride	a bike.
	Meg	can	take	the bus to campus.
	Gary and Jonathan	can	work	in the garden.

Can	Darlene		park	in the garage?	Yes, she can.
Can	I		have	the big bedroom?	No, you can't.
Can	they		find	a cheap house near the beach?	Yes, they can.
Can't	Chrissy		ride	her bike to school?	Yes, she can.
Can't	we		get	a place in the Marina?	No, we can't.
Can't	Bill		take	the small room?	Yes, he can.

	You	can't	find	cheap apartments in Westwood.
	She	can't	ride	her bike on busy streets.
	Meg and Darlene	can't	play	tennis.

Notes

A. Form
   1. The modal CAN does not change for person or number.

   examples   Bill can cook spaghetti.
   Meg and Darlene can speak French.

   2. In negative statements, CAN usually contracts with NOT.

   CANNOT ➡ CAN'T

   examples   We can't find a cheap apartment near campus.
   Jonathan can't gain weight.

B. Position of the modal
   1. In statements, the modal CAN or CAN + NOT comes before the base form of the verb.

   CAN + (NOT) + _____
   (base form of
   the verb)

   examples   Gary can repair cars.
   Darlene can't swim.

   2. In questions, CAN or CAN'T comes before the subject.

   $\begin{Bmatrix} \text{CAN} \\ \text{CAN'T} \end{Bmatrix}$ + _____ + _____
                    (subject)   (base form of
                                  the verb)

   3. Short answers.

   examples   Can't you ride a bike?
                     No, I can't.
                  Can Meg speak French?
                     Yes, she can.

C. Meaning
   1. CAN expresses possibility.

   examples   Meg can take the bus to work.
   They can work in the garden.

2. CAN expresses ability.

   examples   Meg can't play tennis.
   Chrissy can ride a bike.

3. CAN expresses permission.

   examples   Can I have the big bedroom?
   Can Darlene park in the garage?

MASS/COUNT NOUNS

MASS	COUNT
The *food* at the cafeteria is delicious.	I really like the *hamburgers*.
I need some housing *information*.	There are some *notices* on the board.
There's a lot of *traffic* on Washington Blvd.	There are hundreds of *cars* there.
Chrissy has a lot of *homework*.	She has seven *pages* of math *exercises* and a *test* tomorrow.
Let's see how much *money* I have.	I have forty *cents*.

Notes

A. Mass nouns
   1. Mass nouns have no plural form. They take a singular verb.

      examples   The *traffic* is heavy today.
      The *food* here is delicious.

   2. You can talk about the quantity of a mass noun, but you can't use a number immediately before a mass noun. (You can't count it.)

      examples   There's *a lot of* traffic on Lincoln Blvd.
      (quantity)
      Chrissy has *too much* homework tonight.
      (quantity)

B. Count nouns
   1. Count nouns can be singular or plural.

      examples   There's a great *house* for rent in Venice.
      It's 3 *blocks* to the beach.

   2. You can count the quantity of a count noun by using a number before the plural form.

      examples   Gary has *25* students in his class.
      A large Coke is *50* cents.

C. Some nouns can be either mass or count, depending on how you use them.

   examples   Darlene has beautiful long *hair*. (mass)
   Darlene has several gray *hairs*. (count)

   There's a lot of *noise* in the street today. (mass)
   There's *a noise* in the kitchen. (count)

D. The following is a list of some common mass nouns.

ADDITIONAL VOCABULARY: SOME COMMON MASS NOUNS

FLUIDS	SOLIDS	SEMI SOLIDS
water	cheese	shampoo
oil	meat	grease
milk	butter	glue
soup	shortening	catsup
ink	ice	sour cream
beer	ice cream	mayonnaise
wine	glass	peanut butter
tea	iron	honey
coffee	wood	yoghurt
juice	soap	mustard
gasoline	ice	hand cream

SMALL PARTICLES	GASES	NATURAL PHENOMENA
tea	smoke	heat
coffee	smog	weather
salt	air	wind
sugar	oxygen	snow
flour	nitrogen	rain
dust	hydrogen	sunshine
dirt	carbon monoxide	electricity
rice	helium	thunder
cereal	nitrous oxide	humidity

ACADEMIC FIELDS	EMOTIONS, IDEAS & ABSTRACT THOUGHTS	
music	love	laughter
art	hate	kindness
history	anger	cruelty
literature	fun	advice
chemistry	luck	beauty
law	peace	intelligence
business	courage	information
engineering	honesty	pride
medicine	happiness	praise
public health	greed	ridicule

RECREATION	MISCELLANEOUS NOUNS	
baseball	homework	furniture
tennis	traffic	jewelry
golf	skin	underwear
bridge	hair	change [=money]
dancing	paper	luggage
sailing	make-up	baggage

ARTICLES: *A/AN/THE/Ø* (NO ARTICLE)

Meg and Bill are in Brentwood Village. They're looking for an apartment.

Bill: Wait, Meg. I see *a* friend of mine over there.

Meg: Where?

Bill: Over there by *the* market.

Meg: Is he *the* tall dark man or *the* short one?

Bill: He's *the* short one.

Meg: Oh, I see.

Bill: And there's his wife too!

Meg: Is she *the* tiny woman with dark hair?

Bill: Yes.

Meg: They're walking this way.

Bill: George! Carol!

George and Carol: Bill!

George: What are you doing here?

Bill: We're looking for *an* apartment. This is my friend Meg. Meg, these are my friends from *the* tennis club, George and Carol.

Meg: Hi.

George and Carol: Hi.

Bill: Where are you living now?

George: Oh, we have *a* house in *the* suburbs.

Bill: Really? We're looking for *a* house to rent. What's yours like?

George: It has *a* nice yard and *a* big kitchen and three bedrooms.

Bill: Is *the* yard big?

George: No, not too big.

Meg:	We're looking for *a* large house because we have several friends, but it can't be expensive. Are *the* houses in *the* suburbs very expensive?
Carol:	No, they're not too expensive.
Bill:	Let's look at some houses there—maybe we can find *a* large one.
Meg:	But we all want a place near *the* beach, remember?
Bill:	That's true.
George:	Well, we're in a hurry—we still have to get to *the* bank before it closes.
Bill:	Yes, we're going to *the* market before we meet our friends. See you later.
George and Carol:	Okay. . . . nice meeting you, Meg.
Meg:	Nice meeting you too.

Notes

A. Articles with mass and count nouns
    1. Mass nouns sometimes take the definite article THE. They never take the indefinite article A/AN.

       examples   Chrissy hates homework.
                   The homework tonight is very difficult.

    2. Count nouns
      a. Singular count nouns can take A, AN, or THE.

        examples   We're looking for *an* apartment.
                    Is *the* yard big?

      b. Plural count nouns sometimes take THE. They never take A/AN.

        examples   Are *the* houses there expensive?
                    Houses in the suburbs aren't too expensive.

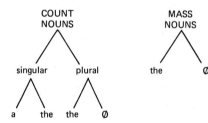

B. Use the indefinite article A/AN when a singular count noun is mentioned or introduced for the first time.

    examples   I see *a* friend of mine over there.
                 We have *a* house in the suburbs.

C. The definite article THE
    1. Use the definite article THE when the noun has been previously mentioned.

FIRST REFERENCE	LATER REFERENCE
It has *a* nice yard.	Is *the* yard big?
Is there *a* pool?	Yes, but *the* pool isn't heated.

2. Use the definite article THE when both the speaker and the listener know something about the noun.

>   **examples**   We have a house in *the* suburbs.
>   *The* campus is beautiful.

>   a. Use the definite article THE when the thing or person is unique, or one of a kind.

>   **examples**   *The* sun is shining today.
>   *The* President is having a press conference today.

>   b. The definite article is frequently used with certain nouns when the speaker and listener share the idea of these nouns.

SHARED IDEAS	
the bank	the doctor
the market	the dentist
the drug store	the university

>   **examples**   I like *the* beach.
>   I'm going to *the* market.

D. Ø (no article): With plural count nouns and mass nouns you don't need to use an article when you talk about the noun in a general way.

>   **examples**   Chrissy hates homework.
>   Cars create smog.

WHERE

>   Where are you from?
>   I'm from Honolulu.
>   Where is the drugstore?
>   It's on the corner of Barrington Avenue and Brentwood Court.
>   Where are we meeting Gary and Jonathan?
>   We're meeting on the pier.
>   Where are Jonathan's parents living?
>   They're living in Boston.

Notes

A. Meaning: The interrogative WHERE asks about location.

>   **examples**   Where are Gary and Jonathan today?
>   They are looking for apartments *in Venice.*
>   (location)
>   Where is Meg working?
>   She's working *on campus.*
>   (location)

B. Position: In information questions WHERE comes at the beginning of the sentence. Note the similarity with the YES/NO question.

>   **examples:**
>   Where ⟦ Are they living in Venice?
>   ⟦ are they living?
>
>   Where ⟦ Is Venice in California?
>   ⟦ is Venice?

C. Responses: The answer to a question with WHERE usually gives a location.

    examples   Where are Darlene and Chrissy living?
                    They're living *in Pasadena.*
                        (location)
            Where is she from?
               Indiana.
            (location)

PREPOSITIONS OF PLACE: WHERE IS _____?

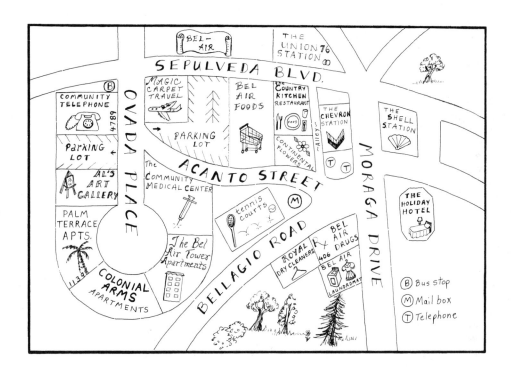

The Holiday Hotel is *in* Bel Air.
There are three service stations *in* Bel Air.

The Holiday Hotel is *on* Moraga Drive.
The Union 76 station is *on* Sepulveda Boulevard.

Community Telephone is *at* 4789 Sepulveda Boulevard.
Bel Air Drugs is *at* 406 Bellagio Road.

Royal Dry Cleaners is *next to* Bel Air Drugs.
There is a restaurant *beside* Bel Air Foods.

The Bel Air Tower Apartments are *between* the Colonial Arms Apartments and the medical center.
The parking lot is *between* Al's Art Gallery and Community Telephone.

Magic Carpet Travel is *at the corner of* Ovada Place and Sepulveda Boulevard.

The mail box is *on the corner of* Acanto Street and Bellagio Road.

The tennis courts are *across the street from* the dry cleaners.

The Shell station is *opposite* the Chevron station.

Notes

A. IN: Use the preposition IN with the name of an area—for example, a neighborhood, a city, a state, or a country.

example
   Bel Air is *in* West Los Angeles.

B. ON: Use the preposition ON with the name of a street.

example
   Continental Flowers is *on* Acanto Street.

C. AT: Use the preposition AT with a specific address.

example
   The Palm Terrace Apartments are *at* 11398 Ovada Place.

D. NEXT TO/BESIDE:

examples
   The Colonial Arms is *next to* the Palm Terrace Apartments.
   There are palm trees *beside* the Palm Terrace Apartments.

E. BETWEEN

example
   The Colonial Arms is *between* the Bel Air Tower Apartments and the Palm Terrace Apartments.

F. $\begin{Bmatrix} AT \\ ON \end{Bmatrix}$ THE CORNER OF

examples

Bel Air Drugs is *on the corner of* Moraga Drive and Bellagio Road.

The mailbox is *at the corner of* Acanto Street and Bellagio Road.

G. ACROSS THE STREET FROM/OPPOSITE

examples

The Holiday Hotel is *across the street from* the laundromat and the pharmacy.

The pharmacy is *opposite* the Holiday Hotel.

QUANTIFIERS: *MUCH/MANY/A LOT OF*

Is there a lot of traffic?
There aren't many apartment buildings in the neighborhood.
There are a lot of old houses on the block.
The area doesn't have much smog.

Notes

A. Meaning: The quantifiers MUCH, MANY, and A LOT OF indicate a large quantity of a noun.

B. Use A LOT OF with mass nouns and plural count nouns. In colloquial speech, LOTS OF is frequently used.

    examples   There's a lot of *smog* today.
(mass
noun)
This block has lots of old *houses.*
(plural count
noun)
The neighborhood doesn't have a lot of *traffic.*
(mass noun)
Is there a lot of *noise?*
(mass noun)

C. Use MANY only with plural count nouns.

    examples   There are many *stores* in the neighborhood.
Many *students* are looking for housing.
Chrissy doesn't have many *friends* in her new school.
Does Meg have many *boyfriends?*

D. Use MUCH only with mass nouns, usually in negative statements and questions.

    examples   We don't have much *time* before dinner.
Santa Monica doesn't have much *smog.*
Is there much closet *space?*

$\begin{Bmatrix} \text{A LOT OF} \\ \text{MUCH} \end{Bmatrix} + \underline{\hspace{3cm}}$
(mass noun)

$\begin{Bmatrix} \text{A LOT OF} \\ \text{MANY} \end{Bmatrix} + \underline{\hspace{3cm}}$
(plural count noun)

COIN	COIN AND BILL NAMES	VALUE		
	a penny	one cent	$ .01	1¢
	a nickel	five cents	$ .05	5¢
	a dime	ten cents	$ .10	10¢
	a quarter	twenty-five cents	$ .25	25¢
	a half dollar a fifty-cent piece	fifty cents	$ .50	50¢
	a dollar bill a one	one dollar	$ 1.00	—
	a five-dollar bill a five	five dollars	$ 5.00	—
	a ten-dollar bill a ten	ten dollars	$10.00	—

Notes

A. U.S. money is usually counted in dollars and cents.

    examples Darlene's telephone bill is twenty-five dollars and sixty-four cents.
                Jonathan has three hundred fifty-two dollars and twenty-eight cents in the bank.

B. MONEY is a mass noun.

    examples I need *some* money for cigarettes.
                    (quantity)
             Meg's parents have *a lot of* money.
                    (quantity)

  1. The names of the coins and bills are count nouns.

      examples I have *three* five-dollar bill*s* and *a* ten-dollar bill.
                  Chrissy has *two* dime*s* and *a* quarter.

C. In conversational English we sometimes omit the words DOLLAR BILL.

    examples I have three *fives* (three five-dollar bills) and a *ten* (a ten-dollar bill).
                We have three *ones* (three one-dollar bills) and two *tens* (two ten-dollar bills).

  1. CENT and DOLLAR are also count nouns.

      examples Darlene's grocery bill is $10.12. (You say: ". . . ten dollars and twelve cents.")

EXERCISE #1. ARTICLES. LEVEL A.

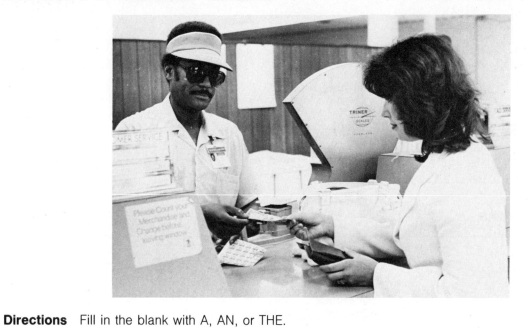

Directions Fill in the blank with A, AN, or THE.

    example *Meg:* I need _____*an*_____ air mail stamp.

At the post office

Clerk: Hi. Can I help you?

Meg: Hi. I have _____ notice about _____ package.
                              (1)   (2)

Clerk: This window is only for stamps. You can pick up _____ package at _____ package
                                                (3)   (4)

      counter over there. Just show _____ notice to _____ clerk.
                                    (5)   (6)

Meg: Oh, but I also need some stamps. Can I get stamps at _____ package counter?
                                                                    (7)

Clerk: No, I can help you with stamps.

Meg: Great. I have _____ air mail letter for Germany, and I need _____ special delivery
                                   (8)   (9)
      stamp.

Clerk: Where's _____ letter to Germany? Let me weigh it. Okay . . . and
                      (10)

      here's _____ special delivery stamp. Is there anything else?
               (11)

Meg: Isn't there _____ new stamp this week?
                     (12)

Clerk: Oh, you mean _____ new commemorative stamp of the Grand Canyon. Here it is.
                    (13)

Meg: That's it. I'll take four.

Clerk: Okay.

Meg: Is there _____ pay phone nearby?
               (14)

Name: _____ Date: _____

Clerk: Yes, there's _____ phone just outside that door over there, but it's frequently broken.
(15)

Meg: Is there another one I can use?

Clerk: Well, yes . . . at _____ drug store across _____ street.
(16) (17)

Meg: Is there _____ xerox machine there too?
(18)

Clerk: No, but there's one at _____ bank next door.
(19)

Meg: Thanks.

Clerk: Don't forget _____ package!
(20

Map of Brentwood Village

EXERCISE #2.   PREPOSITIONS OF PLACE.   PART I.   LEVEL A.

Directions   Look at the map on page 180. Answer each question by completing the sentence.

    example   Where is Village Drugs?

        It is on the corner of _Barrington Avenue_ and _Brentwood Court_ .

        It is next to the _Deli-Delicious Restaurant_ on _Brentwood Court_ .

1. Where is the Wheeler Dealer Bike Shop?

    a. It is in _____ .

    b. It is on _____ .

    c. It is between the _____ and the _____ .

    d. It is at _____ .

2. Where is the Chevron Station?

    a. It's on the corner of _____ and _____ .

    b. It's across the street from _____ .

    c. It's next to _____ on Barrington Avenue.

3. Where is Pets 'N Things?

    a. It's on _____ .

    b. It's between the _____ and the _____ .

    c. It's across the street from _____ .

4. Where's the Shutter Bug Camera Shop?

    a. It's between _____ and _____ .

    b. It's at _____ .

    c. It's on _____ .

5. Where's the United States Post Office?

    a. It's in _____ .

    b. It's next to _____ and _____ on _____ .

    c. It's across the street from _____ and the _____ .

    d. It's at _____ .

EXERCISE #2.   PREPOSITIONS OF PLACE.   PART II.   LEVEL A.

Directions   Look at the map on page 180. Fill in the blanks with the appropriate preposition.

    ON THE CORNER OF / IN / ON / AT / BETWEEN

    OPPOSITE / ACROSS FROM / NEXT TO / BESIDE

    example   Where is the Pastry Chef?

        It is ___*on*___ Brentwood Court.

        It is ___*between*___ the Law Offices and Travel-Wide Tours.

        It is ___*opposite*___ the Brentwood Shop-Easy.

Name: _____   Date: _____

1. Where is Brentwood Motor Inn?

   a. It is _____ Brentwood Village.

   b. It is _____ the post office on Barrington Avenue.

   c. It is _____ Barrington Avenue and Woodbury Place.

2. Where is Rive Gauche Clothing?

   a. It is _____ the park _____ Woodbury Place.

   b. It's _____ the motor inn and the antique store.

   c. It's _____ 1680 Woodbury Place.

3. Where's the Falafel Palace?

   a. It's _____ Village Drugs _____ Barrington Ave.

   b. It's _____ the U.S. Post Office _____ Brentwood Village.

4. Where's the bus stop?

   a. It's _____ Barrington Avenue.

   b. It's _____ Barrington Avenue and Brentwood Court.

   c. It's _____ Village Drugs.

5. Where's the barber shop?

   a. It's _____ the toy store.

   b. It's _____ the law offices and the tailor.

   c. It's _____ 837 Palm Street.

EXERCISE #3. QUANTIFIERS. LEVEL A.

Directions   Look at the following pictures. Choose the correct quantifier and write it in the blank.

example   There isn't _____*any*_____ chance of rain today.
     a. some
     b. many
     c. any

1.

There are _____ types of coffee
     a. several
     b. many
     c. some
at the Coffee Baron.

2.

There aren't _____ apartments
              a. some
              b. much
              c. any
for rent in this building.

3.

There aren't _____ people at
              a. any
              b. many
              c. much
the beach today.

4.

_____ people are standing in
              a. Several
              b. A lot of
              c. Much
line at the Varsity Theatre.

5.

Bill has _____ cans of beer every day.
              a. much
              b. any
              c. several

6.

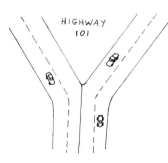

There isn't _____ traffic today.
              a. much
              b. many
              c. any

Name: _____ Date: _____

7.

There's _____ smog today.
   a. many
   b. any
   c. some

8.

Groceries cost _____ money.
   a. many
   b. a lot of
   c. several

9.

Is there _____ homework today?
   a. many
   b. several
   c. much

10.

_____ programs on television
   a. Some
   b. Much
   c. Any
are too violent.

EXERCISE #4. CURRENCY. LEVEL A.

Directions 1. Look at the picture and determine the value of the money.
   2. a. Write the numerical equivalent.
      b. Then write out the sum

example a. _$ 11.35_

   b. _eleven dollars and thirty-_
   five cents

1. a. _____

    b. _____

    _____

2. a. _____

    b. _____

    _____

3. a. _____

    b. _____

    _____

4. a. _____

    b. _____

    _____

5. a. _____

    b. _____

    _____

EXERCISE #5. *CAN.* LEVEL B.

Directions Look at the following pictures. Write a sentence with CAN or CAN'T describing each picture.

example   *Bill can play tennis.*

Name: _____   Date: _____

Jonathan can't ride a horse.

1.

_____

2.

_____

3.

_____

4.

_____

5.

_____

6.

_____

7.

_____

8.

_____

EXERCISE #6.   PREPOSITIONS OF PLACE.   LEVEL B.

Directions   Look at the map on page 180. Write a sentence answering the question. Describe the location with the prepositions given.

example   Where is the Pony Express Bank?
  a. in/ _The Pony Express Bank is in Brentwood Village._
  b. on/ _It's on Palm Street._
  c. on the corner of/ _It's on the corner of Palm Street and Woodbury Place._

Name: _____ Date: _____

1. Where is the Brentwood Shop Easy?

   a. on/ _____

   b. between/ _____

   c. across the street from/ _____

   _____

2. Where is Gutenberg's Books?

   a. in/ _____

   b. on/ _____

   c. between/ _____

3. Where's the Bottle Shop?

   a. on/ _____

   b. next to/ _____

   c. in/ _____

4. Where is the Chevron Station?

   a. on the corner of/ _____

   _____

   b. beside/ _____

   c. opposite/ _____

5. Where is Joe's TV and Electronics?

   a. in/ _____

   b. beside/ _____

   c. at/ _____

EXERCISE #7. PART I. LEVEL C.

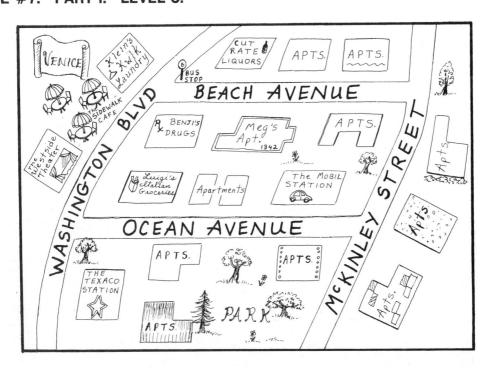

Directions Look at the map on page 188. Then read the following model paragraph.

Meg's apartment is in Venice at 1342 Beach Avenue. There are apartment buildings and small stores and businesses in her neighborhood. The apartment buildings are on Beach Avenue, Ocean Avenue, and McKinley Street. The small businesses are on the main street, Washington Boulevard. Next to Meg's building, on the corner of Beach Avenue and Washington Boulevard, is Benji's Drugs. On the opposite corner, next to the liquor store, there is a bus stop. Luigi's Italian Groceries is next to Benji's Drugs, across from the Westside Theater. Between the theater and Klein's Kwik Laundry is the Sidewalk Cafe. There are also two gas stations and a park in Meg's neighborhood. The Mobil Station is on the corner of McKinley Street and Ocean Avenue. Not far from the park is the Texaco Station on Washington Boulevard. Meg likes the neighborhood, but her apartment building is old and run-down.

EXERCISE #7. PART II. LEVEL C.

Name: _____   Date: _____

Directions Look at the map on page 189. Write a paragraph describing Bill's neighborhood.

_____

_____

_____

_____

_____

_____

_____

_____

_____

_____

_____

_____

_____

EXERCISE #7. PART III. LEVEL C.

Directions Draw a map of your neighborhood in the box on page 190. Write a paragraph describing the neighborhood.

_____

_____

_____

_____

_____

_____

_____

_____

_____

_____

_____

_____

_____

Name: _____ Date: _____

MEETING
THE LANDLORD

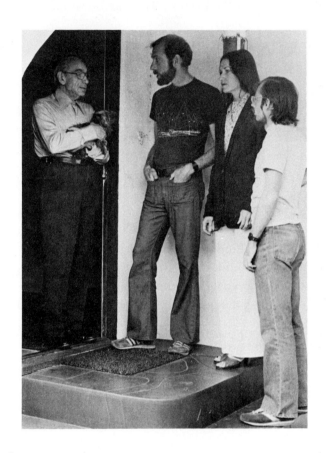

Jonathan knocking at the door

Jonathan: Hello, Mr. Garvey. We're back. These are our friends, Darlene, Chrissy, Meg, and Bill.

Mr. Garvey: Hi. Nice to meet you.

Gary: Can we look at the house?

Mr. Garvey: Sure. Let's see . . . I think I have the key here somewhere. Oh, yes, it's in the kitchen. Just a minute.

Darlene: He seems really nice.

Gary: Yeah, he is. He's a nice man. He's getting old, though. You have to speak up because he can't hear very well.

(landlord returns)

Mr. Garvey: Here are the keys. I think it's this one. The front door is hard to open. You have to pull on the handle and turn the key. Then push.

At the house

Meg:	I like it. There's a lot of room, and it's sunny.
Darlene:	How many bedrooms are there? I can find only four on the second floor.
Gary:	I think there are five. Oh, I remember. The fifth bedroom is really the maid's room. It's on the first floor.
Meg:	Is that the smallest bedroom?
Gary:	No, it's fairly large. The smallest one is upstairs.
Darlene:	How many bathrooms are there? Is there a third one?
Gary:	No, it doesn't have three. It only has two.
Meg:	Do they have tubs?
Gary:	The one upstairs does. It's the biggest. The one downstairs only has a shower.
Meg:	That's okay.
Darlene:	What about the garden? Do we have to take care of it?
Gary:	No, there's a gardener.
Darlene:	Is that an extra cost?
Gary:	No, we don't have to pay for it.
Jonathan:	Hey, there's a fireplace in the living room. Isn't that great?
Chrissy:	Yeah! We can make popcorn!
Darlene:	Well, I really like the house. Can we make a decision today?
Meg:	I like it, too. It's the best house so far.
Jonathan:	And the least expensive!
Meg:	How much is the rent?
Gary:	$850 a month, plus utilities.
Meg:	That's not bad. We can afford that. How much is the deposit?
Gary:	We have to pay the first and last month's rent.
Meg:	Mmm . . . hmm . . . and how many blocks is it to the beach?
Jonathan:	That's the most exciting thing about this house. It's just 3 blocks from the beach. Isn't that fantastic?
Chrissy:	Yeah!
Jonathan:	Well, we have to decide soon. School is starting on Tuesday, and Gary and I don't have a place to live.
Bill:	Let's take it. I like it.
Meg:	So do I.
Jonathan:	Darlene, is it okay with you?
Darlene:	It's fine.
Gary:	Good. Let's go tell Mr. Garvey and sign the lease.

HAVE: SIMPLE PRESENT TENSE

	The house		has	a big kitchen.	
	Meg		has	a job on campus.	
	We		have	a one-year lease.	
Does	the house		have	five bedrooms?	Yes, it does.
Does	Chrissy		have	her own room?	No, she doesn't.
Do	they		have	new tenants?	Yes, they do.
Don't	you		have	a house near the beach?	Yes, I do.
Doesn't	Gary		have	a moustache?	Yes, he does.
Don't	we		have	the keys to the house?	No, we don't.
	I	don't	have	enough money.	
	We	don't	have	a third bathroom.	
	It	doesn't	have	a basement.	

Notes

A. Meaning: The verb HAVE sometimes shows possession. (See Chapter Five.)

B. Form: HAVE is an irregular verb.

  1. Positive statements

      examples   Darlene has a daughter.
                    Florida has a warm climate.
                    Mr. & Mrs. Garvey have a small dog.
                    We have new neighbors.

  2. Negative statements: Use the auxiliary DO/DOES before NOT.

$$\left\{ {DO \atop DOES} \right\} + NOT + \underline{\qquad\qquad}$$
$$\text{(base form of}$$
$$\text{the verb)}$$

      examples   I don't have a job.
                    Gary doesn't have a motorcycle.

    a. The form DOES is used with third person singular subjects.

        examples   Chrissy doesn't have freckles.
                      Meg doesn't have a car.

    b. The form DO is used with all other subjects.

        examples   Meg and Darlene don't have blond hair.
                      The Garveys don't have a swimming pool.

  3. DO/DOES can contract with NOT.

      examples   I don't have time for lunch.
                    Meg doesn't have a car.

  4. Interrogative form: In questions, the auxiliary DO/DOES (+N'T) comes before the subject.

$$\left\{ {DO\,(N'T) \atop DOES\,(N'T)} \right\} + \underline{\qquad\quad} + \underline{\qquad\qquad}$$
$$\text{(subject)}\qquad\text{(base form of}$$
$$\text{verb)}$$

  5. Responses: Use DO/DOES in short answers.

      examples   Do you have an old house?
                  No, we don't.
                  Doesn't Gary have a beard?
                  Yes, he does.

HOW MUCH/HOW MANY WITH THE VERB *BE*

How many bedrooms are there?
    Five.
How much is the rent?
    It's $750 a month.
How much is the deposit?
    The deposit is the last month's rent.
How many blocks is it to the beach?
    Three.

Notes

A. HOW MUCH and HOW MANY are interrogatives. They ask about the cost or quantity of things.

    examples   *How much* are the hot dogs?
                They're *75¢.*
                      (cost)
           How many bathrooms are there?
                Two.
           (quantity)

B. Position: HOW MUCH and HOW MANY come at the beginning of information questions. Notice the similarity with YES/NO question word order.

    examples

                          Are there five bedrooms?
    How many bedrooms | are there?

                          Is the rent $750?
         How much | is the rent?

C. Use HOW MANY with a plural count noun. Sometimes you can omit the noun.

    examples   How many *miles* is it from campus?
                        (plural
                            count noun)
           How many *(people)* are moving into the house?
                    (plural
                        count noun)

D. Use HOW MUCH with a mass noun.

    examples   How much *smog* is there today?
                        (mass
                          noun)
           How much *traffic* is there on the highway?
                    (mass
                        noun)

E. Responses: The answer to a question with HOW MUCH or HOW MANY usually gives the quantity or cost of something.

	QUESTION	RESPONSE
M A S S	How much is the deposit? How much is the ride? How much smog is there today?	The deposit is the last month's rent. 25¢. There's a lot of smog.
C O U N T	How many blocks is it to the beach? How many bedrooms are there? How many cars are there in the parking lot?	It's about 3 blocks to the beach. There are 5 bedrooms. There are a lot of cars in the parking lot.

ADJECTIVES: SUPERLATIVE FORM

Is the bedroom downstairs the smallest one?
It's the best house so far.
And it's the least expensive.
The bathroom upstairs is the biggest one.
That's the most exciting thing about this house.

Notes

A. Use the superlative form of the adjective to show differences between three or more things, persons, or ideas.

    examples   Meg is younger than Darlene, but Chrissy is the youngest.

$$\text{CHRISSY} \quad \overset{\text{young}}{>} \quad \text{MEG} \quad \overset{\text{young}}{>} \quad \text{DARLENE}$$

              Jonathan is shorter than Gary, but Chrissy is the shortest of all.

$$\text{CHRISSY} \quad \overset{\text{short}}{>} \quad \text{JONATHAN} \quad \overset{\text{short}}{>} \quad \text{GARY}$$

  1. Some or all elements of the comparison may be expressed when the superlative is used.

      examples   Jaguars are expensive and BMW's are expensive too, but Rolls Royces are the most expensive.
                  Darlene is older than Meg, but Gary is the oldest.

  2. Sometimes we use a prepositional phrase (". . . of all," ". . . in the . . .") when we talk about a superlative.

      examples   This place is the cheapest *of all.*
                  New York is the largest city *in the U.S.*

B. Form: The definite article THE usually comes before the superlative form.
  1. Form the superlative of most one syllable adjectives by adding -EST.

$$\text{THE} + \underline{\qquad\qquad}\text{-EST}$$
$$\text{(adjective)}$$

    a. With one syllable adjectives, double the final consonant when it comes after a single vowel.

BASE FORM	COMPARATIVE FORM	SUPERLATIVE FORM
short	shorter	shortest
tall	taller	tallest
old	older	oldest
young	younger	youngest
but big	bigger	biggest
fat	fatter	fattest
hot	hotter	hottest
thin	thinner	thinnest

examples   Gary is the tallest in the house.
Jonathan is the smartest of all.

b. Add -EST to two syllable adjectives ending in -Y, -OW, or -ER.   -Y changes to -I before -EST.

BASE FORM	COMPARATIVE FORM	SUPERLATIVE FORM
narrow	narrower	narrowest
shallow	shallower	shallowest
clever	cleverer	cleverest
slender	slenderer	slenderest
but happy	happier	happiest
busy	busier	busiest

examples   Chrissy is the happiest child in her class.
Meg is the prettiest girl.

2. With most other adjectives, form the superlative with MOST or LEAST plus the adjective.

BASE FORM	COMPARATIVE FORM	SUPERLATIVE FORM
careful	more careful	most careful
polite	more polite	most polite
honest	more honest	most honest
intelligent	more intelligent	most intelligent
beautiful	more beautiful	most beautiful
serious	more serious	most serious

examples   Jonathan is the most studious person in the house.
Darlene is the least athletic of all.

3. For some adjectives, the superlative form is irregular.

BASE FORM		COMPARATIVE FORM		SUPERLATIVE FORM
good bad	➡	better worse	➡	best worst
{much many}	➡	more	➡	most
little	➡	less	➡	least

examples   The house on Rose Ave. is the best.
The traffic during rush hour is the worst.

HAVE TO

You have to speak up because Mr. Garvey can't hear very well.
Do we have to take care of the garden?
No, we don't have to pay for it.
You have to pull on the handle and turn the key.

Notes

A. The expression HAVE TO usually shows necessity or obligation.
B. HAVE TO occurs in positive and negative statements and in questions. In conversation, HAVE TO is frequently pronounced as /hæftə/.
C. HAVE TO comes before the base form of the verb.

examples   You have to *speak* loud to Mr. Garvey
(base form
of the verb)
Jonathan has to *move* by Friday.
(base form
of the verb)

D. HAVE TO has the same forms as the main verb HAVE. (See Chapter Seven.)

	We Chrissy		have to has to	move go	by Friday. to a new school.	
Do Does	you Chrissy		have to have to	go change	to work tomorrow? schools?	No, I don't. Yes, she does.
Don't Doesn't	we Chrissy		have to have to	take care of walk	the garden? to school?	No, we don't. Yes, she does.
	You Meg	don't doesn't	have to have to	babysit study	for Chrissy. this weekend.	

ONE/ONES

> This isn't the right key.
> I think it's this one.
> How many bathrooms are there?
> Is there a third one on the first floor?
> There are four bedrooms upstairs.
> The ones in the front have a balcony.
> The small bathroom has a shower and the
> big one has a tub.

Notes

A. **Form:** The noun substitute ONE refers to a singular noun. ONES refers to a plural noun.

examples   The large *key* is for the front door, and the small *one* is for the back door.
The *apartments* near the beach are expensive, but the *ones* near the highway aren't.

B. **Use:** Use the noun substitutes ONE/ONES to replace a previously mentioned count noun.

examples   The old *car* is Gary's, but the new *one* is Bill's.
The *houses* in Venice are old and run-down, but the *ones* in Westwood aren't.

C. ONE/ONES must occur with some form of modification.

examples   That car isn't Gary's. *The gray* one is.
Those aren't my keys. The ones *on the table* are mine.

1. Adjectives and articles (A, AN, and THE) can come before ONE/ONES.

    examples   The classes in the chemistry department are difficult, but *the* ones in biology aren't.
    Isn't *the green* one yours?
    There's *a new* one on the table.

2. The demonstrative adjectives THIS and THAT can modify ONE.

    examples   *This* bedroom is Gary's. *That* one is Jonathan's.
    That bathroom has a tub. *This* one doesn't.

    a. We usually do not use THESE and THOSE before ONES. Use THESE and THOSE alone as pronouns. (See Chapter Six.)

    examples   These papers are Jonathan's. *Those* are Gary's.
    These kids are in Chrissy's class. *Those* aren't.

3. A prepositional phrase can come after ONE/ONES.

    examples   The rooms *in front* are sunny.
    The ones *in back* aren't.

    The car *in the driveway* is Gary's.
    The one *in the street* is Darlene's

4. Ordinal numbers (FIRST, SECOND, THIRD, etc.) and NEXT and LAST can come before ONE/ONES.

    examples   The *second* floor is sunny, but the *first* one isn't.
    The *first* key on the ring is for the front door, and the *next* one is for the basement.

Ordinal numbers

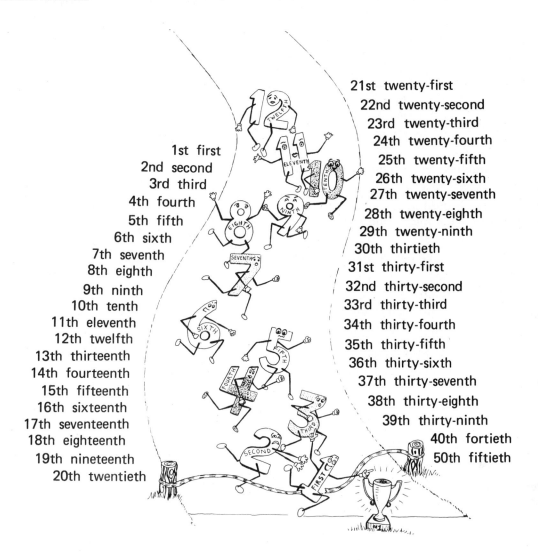

1st first
2nd second
3rd third
4th fourth
5th fifth
6th sixth
7th seventh
8th eighth
9th ninth
10th tenth
11th eleventh
12th twelfth
13th thirteenth
14th fourteenth
15th fifteenth
16th sixteenth
17th seventeenth
18th eighteenth
19th nineteenth
20th twentieth

21st twenty-first
22nd twenty-second
23rd twenty-third
24th twenty-fourth
25th twenty-fifth
26th twenty-sixth
27th twenty-seventh
28th twenty-eighth
29th twenty-ninth
30th thirtieth
31st thirty-first
32nd thirty-second
33rd thirty-third
34th thirty-fourth
35th thirty-fifth
36th thirty-sixth
37th thirty-seventh
38th thirty-eighth
39th thirty-ninth
40th fortieth
50th fiftieth

ORDINAL NUMBERS

Bill's birthday is the 25th of September.
Darlene is meeting Mr. Garvey on September 1st.
Friday the thirteenth is an unlucky day.
Labor Day is on the first Monday of September.
Friday the sixth is moving day.

Notes

A. Form
   1. The ordinals for the numbers ONE, TWO, and THREE are irregular.

CARDINAL NUMBER		ORDINAL NUMBER	
one	(1)	first	(1st)
two	(2)	second	(2nd)
three	(3)	third	(3rd)

2. Some of the other ordinal numbers have irregularities in spelling, but the basic pattern is:

_____-TH
(cardinal number)

CARDINAL NUMBER		ORDINAL NUMBER	
four	(4)	fourth	(4th)
five	(5)	fifth	(5th)
six	(6)	sixth	(6th)

B. Meaning: Ordinal numbers indicate position in a series.

examples   My office is on the sixteenth floor.
Jonathan is third in line.
Let's get off at the second stop.

C. Use
1. Ordinal numbers can come before a noun. (For article usage with noun phrases, see Chapter Seven.)

examples   My bedroom is on the second floor.
Is there a third bathroom?

2. You can use an ordinal number without a noun.

examples   Jonathan is third in line.
In the morning Darlene has coffee first, then she has breakfast.

D. Ordinal number with days and dates of the month
1. Days

$$\left(\frac{}{(day)}\right) + THE + \frac{}{(ordinal)}$$

examples   Monday the second is Labor Day.
The second is Labor Day.

Moving day is the 6th.
Moving day is Friday the 6th.

2. Dates

THE ____ OF ____ ordinal month	____ + (THE) + ____ month ordinal
The third of September is Tuesday. Bill's birthday is the 25th of September. I have a date the 19th of September.	September the third is Tuesday. Bill's birthday is September 25th. I have a date September the 19th.

3. Sometimes the above patterns are combined.

examples   We're moving Friday, the 6th of September.
We're moving Friday, September the 6th.

Wednesday, September 25th, is Bill's birthday.
Wednesday the 25th of September is Bill's birthday.

EXERCISE #1. *HAVE.* LEVEL A.

Directions Fill in the blank with DO(N'T) / DOES(N'T) and HAVE / HAS. Refer to the chart on page 195 if you need help.

example *Mr. Garvey:* I _*have*_ several questions to ask you before you sign the lease.

Mr. Garvey: _____ you _____ any pets?
                (1)   (2)

Darlene: No, we _____.
                      (3)

Mr. Garvey: _____ you all _____ full-time jobs?
                (4)   (5)

Jonathan: Gary _____ a full-time job, but Darlene and I _____ part-time jobs.
                     (6)   (7)
We're students at the university.

Mr. Garvey: What about the other ones—your friends Meg and Bill? _____ Meg
                                                 (8)

_____ a job?
        (9)

Darlene: She's a student too. She _____ a part-time job. And Bill _____
                              (10)   (11)

a full-time job as a tennis teacher in the Marina.

Name: _____ Date: _____

Mr. Garvey: Well, okay then. Let's look at the lease.

Jonathan: Just a minute. We _____ a few questions too.
(12)

Darlene: _____ the house _____ gas or electric heating?
(13)   (14)

Mr. Garvey: It _____ gas heating.
(15)

Darlene: I don't remember . . . _____ it _____ a refrigerator and a stove?
(16)   (17)

Mr. Garvey: It _____ a refrigerator, but it _____ _____ a stove.
(18)   (19)   (20)

Jonathan: Do we _____ to take care of the garden?
(21)

Mr. Garvey: No, you don't. We _____ a gardener.
(22)

Darlene: Sounds great. Let's sign the lease.

EXERCISE #2. *HOW MUCH/HOW MANY.* LEVEL A.

Directions Fill in the blanks with HOW MUCH or HOW MANY.

example *Meg:* _How much_ is the Kona Coffee?
Salesman: It's $6.50 a pound.

Meg: Is there a coffee store in this neighborhood?

Bill: Yeah, there's the Coffee Baron.

Meg: _____ blocks away is it?
                  (1)

Bill: It's just one block away, in the Village.

Meg: Can we go there now? I'm out of coffee at home.

Bill: Sure.

Salesman: Hello. Can I help you?

Meg: I need some coffee.

Salesman: What kind?

Meg: _____ kinds are there?
                  (2)

Salesman: We have 20 different kinds. The special for the week is Mocha Blend.

Meg: _____ is it?
                  (3)

Salesman: $5.50 a pound

Meg: That's too expensive.

Salesman: The House Blend is good, too.

Meg: _____ is it?
                  (4)

Salesman: It's only $4.50 a pound.

Meg: Okay. That's more reasonable.

Salesman: _____ pounds do you want?
                  (5)

Meg: Let's see. I think one pound is enough.

Salesman: Is there anything else today?

Meg: Oh, I also need coffee filters.

Salesman: What size. . . ?

Meg: I'm not sure. _____ sizes are there?
                                (6)

Name: _____   Date: _____

Salesman: We have three sizes . . . for a two-, four-, or six-cup coffee maker. What size is your coffee maker?

Meg: I think it's a four-cup. _____ filters are in a box?
(7)

Salesman: There are fifty per box. _____ boxes do you want?
(8)

Meg: _____ are they?
(9)

Salesman: A box of fifty is $3.75.

Meg: $3.75? Hmm . . . just one box, then.

Salesman: Is that it for today?

Meg: Yes. _____ is the total?
(10)

Salesman: Let's see . . . one pound of House Blend and one box of filters . . . That's $8.75 with tax.

Meg: Here you are.

Salesman: Thank you. Here's your change. Have a nice day.

EXERCISE #3. SUPERLATIVES. LEVEL A.

Directions Read the following dialogue. Fill in the blanks with the superlative form of the adjective.

  example *Darlene:* This is fantastic, Susie.
          Jeff: Yeah. Susie makes the ___*best*___ pizza.
                                         GOOD

Susie: Thanks. It's really easy to make. The dough is from a mix.

Jeff: So, tell us about your new place, Darlene.

Darlene: It's an old five-bedroom house . . . the _____ on the block.
(1) LARGE

The rooms are nice and sunny. There's one small bedroom, but the others are big.

Jeff: Who has the _____ bedroom?
(2) SMALL

Darlene: Meg does. She wants it because it has a balcony.

Susie: Are you all paying the same amount of rent?

Darlene: Yes, but I have the _____ room because of Chrissy.
(3) BIG

Susie: Tell us more about your roommates.

Darlene: Well, there's Meg. She's the _____. She's a friend from my Pennsylvania
(4) YOUNG

days. And then there are three others . . . Gary, Jonathan, and Bill.

Jeff: Gary, Jonathan, and Bill? Hmmm . . . this is getting interesting.

Darlene: We're _just_ roommates. They're all really nice.

Jeff: Are they all students?

Darlene: Only Jonathan . . . and Meg, of course. Jonathan's the _____ and the
(5) STUDIOUS

_____ of the group.
(6) QUIET

Jeff: What do Bill and Gary do?

Darlene: Gary's a third grade teacher. He's the _____ of the group, and Bill is the
(7) OLD

_____. He's a tennis teacher. He's also the _____. He
(8) ATHLETIC   (9) BUSY

has lots of girlfriends, and he's never home.

Susie: That's the _____ type of roommate!
(10) GOOD

Darlene: I agree, but Bill is also the _____ and the _____ . . .
(11) NOISY   (12) MESSY

and that's the _____ type of roommate.
(13) BAD

Susie: Lucky for you he's never home.

Darlene: Yeah.

Susie: Is Chrissy happy with the new situation?

Darlene: Oh, it's perfect for her. She has three fathers now, but she's the _____
(14) COMFORTABLE

with Gary because he likes kids. He's the _____ too. Jonathan and Bill aren't
(15) PATIENT

used to kids.

Susie: Well, I'm so happy that everything is working out so well.

Darlene: So am I.

Name: _____   Date: _____

EXERCISE #4. *ONE/ONES.* LEVEL A.

Directions Fill in the blanks with ONE or ONES.

example   *Chrissy:*   Is this the house?
                 Jonathan: No, it's the _____*one*_____ across the street.

Jonathan: Excuse me, Mr. Garvey. Is this the key to the front door?

Mr. Garvey: No, that's not the right _____. The front door key is the small _____ at
                   the end.   (1)   (2)

Jonathan: What about the back-door and basement keys?

Mr. Garvey: Let me see. They're the small _____ in the middle. The basement key is the
                                         (3)

              green _____ and the back-door key is the silver _____.
                       (4)   (5)

Darlene: I like the houses on this street. They're old, but they're not run-down.

Mr. Garvey: Yeah, this is a nice block. Some of the houses in the area are run-down, but the _____
              on this block aren't.   (6)

Darlene: Oh, these rooms are nice and big. Are the bedrooms big too?

Mr. Garvey: Three of the bedrooms upstairs are large, and so is the _____ downstairs. The
                                                        (7)

              fourth _____ upstairs is small, but it has a balcony . . . both of the front bedrooms
                         (8)

              have balconies. They're beautiful rooms . . . nice and sunny . . . oh, yes, and the

              _____ downstairs has a separate entrance.
                    (9)

Chrissy: Are there any kids in the neighborhood?

Mr. Garvey: Let's see. The family next door has two twin girls, and the _____ across the
                street has a little boy.   (10)

Chrissy: That's great! Are they my age?

Mr. Garvey: I don't know. How old are you?
Chrissy: I'm 7.

Mr. Garvey: Hmm . . . Well, the kids next door are just starting school, but the _____ across
                the street is about your age. He's in the second grade, I think.   (11)

Darlene: Does the house have only one bathroom?

Mr. Garvey: No, it has two. The master bathroom is upstairs, but there's a small _____ downstairs.
Darlene: It's perfect. Let's find the others and talk about the lease.   (12)

EXERCISE #5. ORDINAL NUMBERS. LEVEL A.

Darlene's calendar

DECEMBER

SUNDAY	MONDAY	TUESDAY	WEDNESDAY	THURSDAY	FRIDAY	SATURDAY
					1 term paper due	2 7:30pm dinner with Al
3 study all day!	4 Final Exam Week →	5 3:00pm Poli Sci final	6 work evening!	7 study all day	8 11:30am Philosophy Exam drinks with Meg	9 Christmas Shopping
10 Mom's birthday	11 Semester break begins →	12 take the car in for its 18,000 mile check	13 work all day	14	15	16 Christmas Shopping
17	18 Chrissy's vacation begins →	19	20 2:30pm Chrissy's doctor appointment	21	22 office party	23 9:00 Meg's party
24 Chrissy's birth-day party New Year's Eve 31	25 CHRISTMAS DAY	26 shopping - after Christmas sales!	27	28	29	30

Directions   Look at the above calendar. Use the patterns below to fill in the blanks in the following sentences.
Write out the ordinal numbers.

THE _____ + OF + _____
　　　　　ordinal　　　　　　　　　month

_____ + (THE) + _____
　　month　　　　　　　　　ordinal

_____ + THE + _____
　　day　　　　　　　　　ordinal

example   Wednesday the ___*thirteenth*___ Darlene has to work all day.

Name: _____   Date: _____

1. The _____ and seventh _____ December, Darlene has to study all day.

2. She has final exams Tuesday the _____ and Friday the _____.

3. Darlene is meeting Al Saturday _____ _____.

4. She has a term paper due Friday the _____.

5. The beginning of semester break is Monday _____ _____.

6. There's an office party Friday the _____-_____ of _____.

7. Darlene is doing her Christmas shopping Saturday _____ ninth and Saturday _____ sixteenth.

8. _____ _____ of December, Darlene has to take her car in for the 18,000 mile check-up.

9. There's a New Year's Eve party Sunday _____ _____

   _____.

10. Christmas is _____ _____-_____ _____

   _____.

EXERCISE #6. *HAVE.* LEVEL B.

Directions   Read the following telephone conversation between Meg and her mother. Using the verb HAVE, write Mrs. Bernstein's questions.

   example   *Mom:*   <u>*Do you have a new apartment*</u>?
                 Meg: No, we don't have a new apartment.

Meg: Hi, Mom. How are things?

Mom: Everything's fine here. How are you?

Meg: I'm fine. I have good news. I'm moving on Friday.

Mom: That's great!

_____?
(1)

Meg: Yes, I have some roommates.
Mom: How many?
Meg: Four.
Mom: Four roommates!

_____?
(2)

Meg: Yes, we have a house. It's a five-bedroom place in Venice.

Mom: _____?
(3)

Meg: Yes, I have my own bedroom.

Mom: _____?
(4)

Meg: Yes, the house has a yard.
Mom: That's great, but isn't Venice expensive?
Meg: No, it isn't. It's near the beach, but the houses are old.

Mom: _____?
(5)

Meg: Sure, I have enough money. The rent is only $170 each.

Mom: _____?
(6)

Meg: Yes, it has a garage.
Mom: Is the house far from campus?
Meg: It's about five or six miles.
Mom: What about transportation?
Meg: Oh, I can take the bus or go with Darlene.

Mom: _____?
(7)

Meg: Yes, she has a car.
Mom: Tell me more about your roommates.

_____?
(8)

Meg: Yes, they all have jobs. Two are teachers, and the others are students with part-time jobs.
Mom: That's nice.
Meg: Well, I have to go. This call is costing too much.
Mom: Okay, call again soon.
Meg: Okay, Mom. Bye.

Name: _____ Date: _____

Directions   Write Darlene's questions. Use WHERE, WHAT, HOW MUCH, and HOW MANY.

      example   *Darlene:*   <u>Where is the house</u> ?
                Jonathan: It's in Venice.

Darlene: Tell me about the house.

Jonathan: It's perfect. It has everything.

Darlene: _____?
                                 (1)

Jonathan: There are five bedrooms.

Darlene: _____?
                                 (2)

Jonathan: The rent is only $850 a month.

Darlene: _____?
                                 (3)

Jonathan: The deposit is $850.

Darlene: _____?
                                 (4)

Jonathan: It's near the beach in Venice.

Darlene: _____?
                                 (5)

Jonathan: The name of the street is Rose Avenue.

Darlene: _____?
                                 (6)

Jonathan: It's about three blocks to the beach.

Darlene: _____?
                                 (7)

Jonathan: There isn't a lot of traffic. The street is really quiet.

Darlene: _____?

                                    (8)

Jonathan: The landlord's name is Mr. Garvey.

Darlene: The place sounds great. Let's go see Mr. Garvey.

EXERCISE #8.   SUPERLATIVES.   LEVEL B.

Directions   Look at the following pictures. Write three sentences for each picture.
a. Use an adjective.
b. Use the comparative form.
c. Use the superlative form.

example   tall
a. *Chrissy is tall.*
b. *Darlene is taller.*
c. *Gary is the tallest of all.*

1.    young
a. _____
b. _____
c. _____

2.    IMPORTED BEER PRICES   expensive
a. _____
b. _____
c. _____

3. 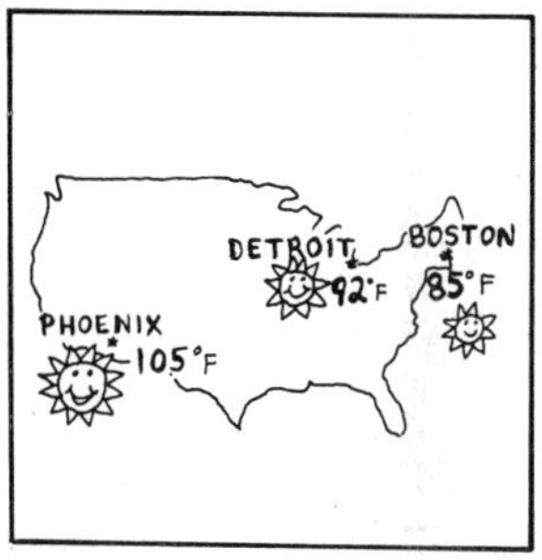   hot
a. _____
b. _____
c. _____

Name: _____   Date: _____

4.

INCHES OF
RAIN PER YEAR 66.9

59.8

54.6

JUNEAU   MIAMI   MOBILE

rainy

a. _____

b. _____

c. _____

5.

RESTAURANT GUIDE
☆
NAME OF RESTAURANT	RATING
La Maison de Cuisine	★ ★ ★
Au Bon Appetit	★ ★ ★ ★
Le Repas Royal	★ ★ ★ ★ ★

good

a. _____

b. _____

c. _____

EXERCISE #9. *ONE/ONES.* LEVEL B.

Directions Write a sentence using BE or HAVE with the information given below. Use ONE or ONES to replace the second noun.

example

Gary   **Jonathan**

short man / Jonathan
tall man / Gary

The short man is Jonathan, and the tall one is Gary.

1.

Royce Hall   **Bunche Hall**

Royce Hall / old building
Bunche Hall / modern building

_____

2.

New York   **Tamaqua**

New York / large city
Tamaqua / small city

_____

3.

Mercedes   **Volkswagen**

rich men / Mercedes
poor men / Volkswagens

_____

4.

Leonardo's Shoe Gallery / expensive shoes
Shoes Unlimited / cheap shoes

_____

_____

5.

Meg   **Darlene**

Meg / new clothes
Darlene / old clothes

_____

Name: _____   Date: _____

6.

The inner-city   **The suburbs**

the suburbs / well-kept houses
the inner-city / run-down houses

___

7.

Rose Avenue   **Sepulveda Boulevard**

Sepulveda Boulevard / a noisy street
Rose Avenue / a quiet street

___

8.

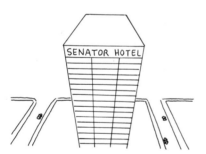 

the 18-story building / the Senator Hotel
the 3-story building / the Camden Motor Inn

___

EXERCISE #10.   ORDINAL NUMBERS.   LEVEL B.

Darlene's calendar

SEPTEMBER

SUNDAY	MONDAY	TUESDAY	WEDNESDAY	THURSDAY	FRIDAY	SATURDAY
1 beach picnic	2 LABOR DAY	3 shopping with Chrissy	4 pick up the house keys	5 clean the house	6 MOVING DAY!	7
8	9 call the telephone company	10 the 1st day of school for Chrissy	11	12 work late	13 bad luck!	14
15 visit Aunt Mildred	16	17	18	19 dentist appointment	20	21 go camping →
22 → camping	23 meet Meg for dinner	24	25 Bills' birthday	26	27	28
29	30 pay rent!					

Directions   Look at Darlene's calendar. Write a sentence using the ordinal patterns and the information given below. Use the present progressive tense.

THE + _____ + OF + _____
　　　　　　　ordinal　　　　　　　　　month

_____ + (THE) + _____
　month　　　　　　　　　　ordinal

_____ + THE + _____
　day　　　　　　　　　ordinal

example   (pick up the keys from Mr. Garvey)

Darlene is picking up the keys from Mr. Garvey Wednesday the fourth.

1. (go to the dentist) _____

_____

2. (pay the rent) _____

_____

3. (celebrate Bill's birthday) _____

_____

4. (work late) _____

_____

Name: _____   Date: _____

5. (have a picnic at the beach) _____

_____

6. (clean the house) _____

_____

7. (meet Meg for dinner) _____

_____

8. (call the telephone company) _____

_____

9. (go shopping with Chrissy) _____

_____

10. (go camping) _____

_____

EXERCISE #11. PART I. LEVEL C.

Directions Look at Bill's schedule. Then read the model paragraph.

Bill's schedule

SEPTEMBER	SUNDAY 1
	10 a.m. - private lesson with Mrs. Johnson 12 a.m. - lunch with Judy 1:30 - 5:30 - group lessons 7:30 p.m. - pick up Carol

MONDAY 2	TUESDAY 3
a.m. beach with Cheryl evening - Cheryl ?? LABOR DAY	10-12 a.m. - private lessons with Mrs. Andrews 1:30 - 3:00 - Mrs. Thompson and Mrs. Granger 3:30 - 4:00 - lesson with Billy DINNER WITH JANE

WEDNESDAY 4	THURSDAY 5
1 - 5 pm - group lessons 6 pm - call Debbie 7:30 - date with Susie	a.m. - sailing with Ann 3 - 4 pm - teach kids 7 pm - dinner with Cheryl

FRIDAY 6	SATURDAY 7
MOVING DAY !!	teach all day ☹ 6 pm - call Debbie evening - movies with Joyce

Bill has a lot of dates this week. He has a date with Carol on the first, and he's spending all day Monday the second with Cheryl. He's also going to dinner with Cheryl on Thursday the fifth. He doesn't have to teach on Monday the second because it's Labor Day, and he's not teaching on Friday because he's moving. He has to teach all day on the first and the seventh because a lot of people have their lessons on the weekend. He has many adult students and a few children. This week he has several private lessons: Mrs. Andrews has her lesson on the third, and Mrs. Johnson has one on the first. Bill has a full schedule. He's always very busy.

EXERCISE #11. PART II. LEVEL C.

Directions Look at Meg's schedule. Write a paragraph about Meg's week.

Meg's schedule

SEPTEMBER	SUNDAY 1
	beach picnic with Darlene and Chrissy
MONDAY 2	TUESDAY 3
go bike riding with Mike	work all day / dinner with Sam
LABOR DAY	
WEDNESDAY 4	THURSDAY 5
find boxes and pack	clean the house
FRIDAY 6	SATURDAY 7
move into the house in Venice	unpack and relax

_____

_____

_____

_____

_____

_____

_____

_____

_____

_____

Name: _____ Date: _____

_____
_____
_____
_____
_____
_____
_____
_____
_____
_____
_____
_____
_____
_____
_____
_____
_____

EXERCISE #11. PART III. LEVEL C.

Directions Fill in the calendar below with your schedule for the week. Then write a paragraph describing your week.

Your schedule

(month)	SUNDAY	1
MONDAY 2	TUESDAY	3
WEDNESDAY 4	THURSDAY	5
FRIDAY 6	SATURDAY	7

Name: _____   Date: _____

MOVING DAY

At the house

Meg:	When are Jonathan and Gary arriving?
Darlene:	I don't know.
Chrissy:	Look, Mommy. Here they are. They're coming into the driveway.
Darlene:	Let's go help unload the truck.
Meg:	Hi, Gary. Hi, Jonathan. Where's Bill?
Gary:	He has a tennis lesson this morning.
Meg:	When is he coming?
Gary:	At 11:30.
Meg:	Are his things on the truck?
Gary:	We have some of his furniture. There are a lot of boxes in his bedroom already.
Jonathan:	Let's start. We only have the truck until six tonight. Chrissy, here—take the key and go open the door, please.
Darlene:	There are some things in my car. Meg, let's unload the car first. Gary and Jonathan can start with the truck.

Chrissy: Jonathan, I need help! I'm having trouble. I can't open the door.

Jonathan: Yeah, the door sticks. Turn the key and pull the door. Then push.

Chrissy: Oh, okay. It's open.

Jonathan: That's great, Chrissy. Now go help your mother and Meg unload the car.

Gary: Wait, Chrissy. Take this lamp.

Chrissy: Whose is it?

Gary: I think it belongs to Meg.

Meg: (coming outside) Oh, yeah. That's all mine. Put it in my bedroom upstairs. Don't drop it. Be careful.

Gary: Whose bed is this?

Meg: That's Darlene and Chrissy's.

Darlene: Oh, yeah. That's ours.

Gary: It weighs a ton!

Jonathan: It's really nice. It looks antique.

Darlene: Yeah, it is. It's my aunt's. She has a lot of antique furniture, but she lives in a condominium now and doesn't have room for it. Chrissy and I are using a lot of her furniture. Where *is* Chrissy? Chrissy?

Chrissy: I'm in here—in Bill's room.

Darlene: What are you doing?

Chrissy: I'm looking at Bill's stuff. He keeps everything! Look at all this junk.

Darlene: Don't be nosy. Come in here and help us.

THE SIMPLE PRESENT TENSE: PART I

THIRD PERSON SINGULAR FORM (HE, SHE, IT FORM)	OTHER FORMS
The door sticks.	I need help.
It belongs to Meg.	I think that's mine.
This bed weighs a ton!	My parents live in Boston.
It looks antique.	We like our new place.
She lives in a condominium.	Meg and I hate housework.
He keeps everything.	You watch a lot of television.

Notes

A. Positive statement form

   1. The third person singular form is the uninflected verb form plus -S.

     examples She leaves her toys everywhere.
                       Bill hates housework.

   2. The uninflected verb form is used in all other cases.

     examples I leave my clothes everywhere.
                       We hate housework.
                       Gary and Jonathan watch television after dinner.

B. Use

   1. Use the simple present tense to describe habitual actions or events.

examples   Nobody washes the dishes.
               Gary burns everything.
               Every Monday I work late.

2. Use the simple present tense with certain verbs to describe states or conditions. (See Chapter Six.)
   a. Some verbs in this group are:
      WANT   NEED   LIKE   SEEM   HATE   HAVE   KNOW   BELIEVE
      APPEAR   LOVE   (=own)

     examples   I want a new car.
                    Darlene needs a babysitter.
                    Meg hates housework.
                    The landlord seems nice.
                    Jonathan has a motorcycle.
                    Bill likes spaghetti.

3. Use the simple present tense with certain verbs of sensory perception.
   a. Some verbs in this group are:
      SEE   HEAR   SMELL   TASTE   FEEL

     examples   I see Chrissy. She's behind the house.
                    I smell dinner. It's almost ready.
                    I hear Bill's stereo. It's too loud.

4. Use the simple present tense to express general truths.

     examples   Vegetarians never eat meat.
                    The sun rises in the east and sets in the west.

C. Spelling irregularities
   1. When the base form of the verb ends in -O or in a "hissing" sound as represented by the letters -X, -SS, -CH, -TCH, -SH, -Z, or -ZZ add -ES to the third person singular form.

O	Meg g*oes* shopping with Darlene.
X	Jonathan fi*xes* his motorcycle.
SS	Sometimes Meg mi*sses* the bus.
CH	Gary tea*ches* third grade.
TCH	Chrissy wa*tches* television in the evening.
SH	Nobody wa*shes* the dishes.
ZZ	The alarm clock bu*zzes* at 6 A.M.

2. When the base form of the verb ends in a consonant plus -Y, the -Y changes to -I before -ES to form the third person singular.

BASE FORM	3rd PERSON SINGULAR
cry	cries
try	tries
dry	dries

but

BASE FORM	3rd PERSON SINGULAR
play	plays
stay	stays
say	says

examples   Chrissy tr*ies* her best in school.
Bill dr*ies* the dishes after dinner.
Chrissy pla*ys* softball with Gary after school.

POSSESSIVE PRONOUNS

Is this stuff yours?
No, it's theirs.
That's all mine.
Are the things on the truck his?

Notes

A. Possessive pronouns show possession or a close relationship. They do not occur with a noun.

examples   The bed is *ours.*
That's *mine.*

B. Form

	SINGULAR	PLURAL
1st person	mine	ours
2nd person	yours	yours
3rd person	his hers its	theirs

C. Use: A possessive pronoun can take the place of a noun phrase.

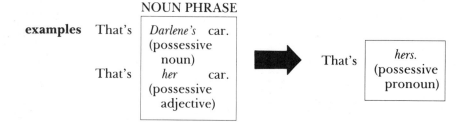

NOUN PHRASE

examples   That's   *Darlene's* car.
(possessive noun)

That's   *her* car.
(possessive adjective)

→ That's   *hers.*
(possessive pronoun)

WHEN

When are Jonathan and Gary arriving?
     They're arriving in a few minutes.
When is Bill coming?
     At 11:30.
When do you have to return the truck?
     At six.
When does Bill have his tennis lesson?
     From ten to eleven.

Notes

A. Meaning: The interrogative pronoun WHEN asks about time.

    examples   When is Bill coming?
                At 11:30.
                  (time)
            When are you moving?
                On Friday.
                  (time)

B. Position: WHEN comes at the beginning of information questions. Notice the similarity with YES/ NO question word order.

    examples

When	Does Bill have a tennis lesson this morning?
	does Bill have a tennis lesson?
When	Is he coming at 11:30?
	is he coming?

C. Responses: The answer to a WHEN question usually gives a time.

    examples   When is moving day?
                It's *on Friday.*
                  (time)
            When are they coming?
                Soon.
            (time)

PREPOSITIONS OF TIME: *IN, ON, AT, FROM . . . TO, UNTIL*

Jonathan and Gary are arriving in a few minutes.
Bill's coming at 11:30.
We only have the truck until six tonight.
His tennis lesson is from ten to eleven.

Notes

A. IN: The preposition IN is used with blocks of time.

IN + _____ (daily time period)	IN + ____ (month)
in the morning	in January
in the afternoon	in June
in the evening	in September
IN + ____ (year)	**IN + ____ (season)**
in 1948	in fall
in 1814	in winter
in 2001	in spring
in 1776	in summer

    examples   Jonathan works on his thesis in the morning.
                  Sometimes he jogs at the beach in the afternoon.

1. Use time expressions with IN to talk about the future.

   examples He's leaving for school in 10 minutes.
   I'm graduating from college in two months.

2. Position: Time expressions with IN can come at the beginning or end of a sentence.

   examples He's usually free in the evening.
   In the evening he's usually free.

B. ON
   1. Meaning
      a. Use the preposition ON before a specific day or date. You can also omit ON.

         examples Chrissy has a dental appointment (on) Monday.
         My mother's birthday is (on) June 6th.

      b. Use the preposition ON to talk about a habitual activity.

         ON + _____   =   EVERY + _____
              (name of   (name of
              day+s)   day)

         examples I have class *on* Tuesday*s*.
         (=I have class *every* Tuesday.)
         I study in the library *on* Monday*s*.
         (=I study in the library *every* Monday.)

      c. ON TIME means "punctual."

         examples Bill is never on time.
         Be on time, please.

   2. Position: Time expressions with ON can come at the beginning or end of a sentence.

      examples He plays tennis on Sundays.
      On Sundays he plays tennis.

C. AT: Use the preposition AT before a specific time.

   examples Jonathan eats breakfast at 7 o'clock.
   At one o'clock he eats lunch.

   1. Other expressions of time with AT:

      at noon   at night   at once (=immediately)
      at midnight   at the moment   at sunset
                                        at sunrise

      examples At night he likes to watch television.
      Jonathan teaches at noon.

D. FROM . . . TO: The pattern FROM . . . TO gives the beginning and end of a period of time.
   1. FROM gives the beginning of the time period.
   2. TO gives the end of the time period.

      examples Jonathan has his physics lab from 8 o'clock to 12 o'clock on Monday.
      He studies from nine to one on Saturday.

   3. Position: The pattern FROM . . . TO usually comes in the middle or at the end of a sentence.

      examples He always works on his thesis from eight to eleven on Tuesday and Thursday.
      He has an astronomy lecture from two to five on Tuesdays.

E. UNTIL: The preposition UNTIL gives the end of a time period.

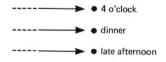

examples We have the truck until six this evening.
Chrissy's at school until late afternoon.

1. Position: Time expressions with UNTIL usually come in the middle or at the end of a sentence.

examples Jonathan studies until midnight because he wants good grades.
Meg works until five o'clock.

IMPERATIVES

Put it in my bedroom upstairs.
Take this lamp and put it in Meg's bedroom.
Don't break it.

Don't be nosy.
Go open the door.
Let's not sit around. Let's start.

Notes

A. The simple imperative
  1. Meaning: Use the imperative to give a command or to make a suggestion to the listener.

examples Answer the telephone.
Put that box in the corner.

  2. Form
    a. Positive imperative form: The imperative form is the base form of the verb. The subject (you) is not used.

examples: *Go* home! *Open* the door.
(base form) (base form)

    b. Negative imperative form: In the negative imperative form, the base form of the verb comes after DO NOT or DON'T.

$$\left\{\begin{matrix} \text{DON'T} \\ \text{DO NOT} \end{matrix}\right\} \; + \; \underline{\qquad\qquad\qquad}$$
(base form of the verb)

examples Don't be nosy.
Don't break anything.

    c. You can use PLEASE before an imperative to be more polite.

examples Please take out the trash.
Please don't play your stereo.

B. The GO-imperative
  1. Meaning: The GO-imperative usually involves movement.

examples Go get the keys in the kitchen.
Go move your motorcycle.

  2. Form: GO comes before the base form of the verb.

$$\text{GO} \; + \; \underline{\qquad\qquad\qquad}$$
(base form of the verb)

examples Go find Meg.
Go start dinner.

C. The LET'S imperative is an invitation or suggestion which includes the speaker and the listener(s).

examples We're all here now. Let's start.
Let's carry these boxes upstairs.

  1. With certain action verbs, you can use the imperative form LET'S GO plus the -ING form of the verb.

examples Let's go swimming after lunch.
Let's go camping this weekend.

PREPOSITIONS OF PLACE

Review

1.

IN
There's a fireplace in the living room.
Meg's TV set is in the living room too.

2.

ON
Darlene's plants are on the balcony.
Darlene is lying on a chaise lounge.

3.

AT
There's someone at the door.
We live at 1843 Rose Avenue.

More prepositions

4.

$\left\{\begin{array}{l}\text{BEHIND}\\\text{IN BACK OF}\end{array}\right\}$ / IN FRONT (OF)

There's a garage $\left\{\begin{array}{l}\text{in back of}\\\text{behind}\end{array}\right\}$ the house.

Darlene's car is in front of the house.

5.

UPSTAIRS / DOWNSTAIRS
Bill's bedroom is downstairs.
The big bathroom is upstairs.

6.

UNDER
There are cupboards under the counter.
Let's keep the garbage can under the sink.

7.

OVER, ABOVE
There's a mirror above the fireplace.
There's an old chandelier over the dining room table.

8.

AGAINST
Darlene's piano is against the wall.
There are bookcases against the wall.

EXERCISE # 1.   THE SIMPLE PRESENT TENSE.   LEVEL A.

Directions   In the following blanks, fill in the correct present tense form of the verb. Be careful with spelling
irregularities.

example   *Chrissy:*   Bill ____*keeps*____ everything.
                                    KEEP

Darlene: He ____*has*____ a lot of things, but I'm sure he
                           HAVE

____*throws*____ a lot of things away too.
      THROW

Chrissy: Bill sure _____ a lot of junk.
                              (1) HAVE

Darlene: That _____n't junk. Those _____ Bill's personal possessions.
                         (2) BE   (3) BE

Chrissy: It _____ like junk to me.
                    (4) LOOK

Darlene: Maybe it _____ like junk to you, but I _____ sure it
                          (5) LOOK   (6) BE

_____ important to Bill.
      (7) BE

Chrissy: But he _____ strange things . . . for example, under his bed he
                        (8) KEEP

_____ tennis rackets. He never _____ them.
      (9) HAVE   (10) FIX

Darlene: . . . broken tennis rackets?

Chrissy: Yeah, and he _____ piles of dirty clothes all over the room.
                             (11) LEAVE

Darlene: Hmm . . .

Name: _____   Date: _____   **233**

Chrissy: And his room _____ like cigarettes because every night he _____
                      (12) SMELL   (13) WATCH

        television and _____ in bed. He never _____ the ashtrays.
                        (14) SMOKE   (15) EMPTY

Darlene: He probably _____ cleaning. Besides, he doesn't have much time.
                      (16) HATE

        He _____ every day.
            (17) TEACH

Chrissy: Yeah, and he _____ all his free time with his girlfriends.
                      (18) SPEND

Darlene: Well, you _____ your free time with your friends, and you never
                  (19) SPEND

        _____ up your room.
           (20) CLEAN

Chrissy: That _____ different. I _____ just a kid, and kids
               (21) BE   (22) BE

        _____ play time. Besides, Bill _____ every day.
           (23) NEED   (24) PLAY

Darlene: He _____ tennis, but that _____ his work.
              (25) PLAY   (26) BE

Chrissy: I _____. He _____ to work. At work, he _____
       (27) UNDERSTAND   (28) GO   (29) WORK

        and he _____ at the same time.
             (30) PLAY

Darlene: Very clever.

EXERCISE #2. POSSESSIVES. LEVEL A.

Directions Fill in the blank with the correct possessive pronoun.

    example   Darlene and Chrissy have a front bedroom.
                Meg's bedroom is next to _*theirs*_____.

1. *Chrissy:*   Do we have the small bedroom or the large one?

   Darlene: The large one is _____ and the small one is Meg's.

2. *Bill:*   Chrissy, don't be nosy. That isn't your stuff. It's _____.

3. *Chrissy:*   Jonathan and Gary, is that your truck?

   Jonathan: No, it isn't _____. It's a rental truck.

4. *Chrissy:*   Bill, which bedroom is _____?
   Bill: My bedroom is downstairs, next to the kitchen.

5. *Meg:*   Bill, is that beautiful brass bed _____?
   Bill: No, it belongs to Darlene. It was her aunt's.
   Meg: Is that her brass lamp too?
   Bill: Yes, I think it's _____.

6. *Jonathan:*   Is that Mr. Garvey's car in our driveway?
   Gary: No, _____is that old one across the street.

7. *Chrissy:*   The twins next door are really lucky.
   Darlene: Why?

   Chrissy: Well, I like our house, but _____ has a swimming pool.

8. *Jonathan:*   Is that Mr. Garvey's dog?
   Chrissy: No, that's the neighbor's dog.
   Jonathan: Isn't Mr. Garvey's dog a poodle?

   Chrissy: No, _____ is a Yorkshire Terrier.

EXERCISE #3.   INTERROGATIVES.   LEVEL A.

Directions   Fill in the blank with the correct interrogatives:
WHO   WHOSE   WHAT   WHEN   WHERE   WHY.

example   *Meg:*   _____*When*_____'s Bill coming?
            Gary: At 11:30.

Meg: _____'s Chrissy?
                        (1)

Jonathan: I think she's upstairs in your bedroom.

Meg: _____ is she in my bedroom?
                        (2)

Jonathan: Because she's nosy. She's probably snooping in your things.

Meg: _____'s Darlene?
                        (3)

Jonathan: She's at the market. She's getting some food for lunch.

Name: _____   Date: _____

Meg: I hope she's not away too long. That kid is driving me crazy.

Chrissy: Meg, _____'s this?
                        (4)

Meg: It's my diary. Chrissy, put that back. It's private.

Chrissy: _____?
               (5)

Meg: In my bedroom, in the box with all my papers.

Chrissy: _____'s Mommy coming back?
               (6)

Jonathan: In a few minutes.

Chrissy: I'm starving. _____ can I eat?
                                (7)

Meg: Nothing. Wait until your Mommy returns.

Chrissy: _____ cookies are these?
               (8)

Jonathan: They're mine.

Chrissy: Can I have one?

Meg: No.

Chrissy: _____ not?
               (9)

Meg: Because cookies spoil your appetite.

Jonathan: Chrissy, go find Gary.

Chrissy: _____ is he?
               (10)

Jonathan: He's outside in the garage.

Chrissy: _____ is he in the garage?
               (11)

Jonathan: He's unpacking some things.

Chrissy: Oh, okay.

Meg: Good work. Now she can bother Gary for awhile.

Chrissy: I can't find Gary. He's not in the garage. _____ is he?
                                                                 (12)

Jonathan: Oh, that's right. He's with Darlene at the market.

Chrissy: _____ are they coming back?
               (13)

Meg: In a few more minutes.

Chrissy: _____ is it taking so long?
               (14)

Meg: Because the markets are always busy on Friday.

Jonathan: _____'s that? I think there's a car coming in the driveway. Chrissy, go check.
               (15)

Chrissy: It's Mommy and Gary. They're back!

Meg: At last!

Jonathan's schedule

September

TIME	MONDAY	TUESDAY	WEDNESDAY	THURSDAY	FRIDAY	SATURDAY	SUNDAY
7:00	breakfast	breakfast	breakfast	breakfast	breakfast		
8:00	physics lab	work on Thesis		work on Thesis			
9:00			physics discussion		physics discussion	study	tennis with Bill
10:00							buy newspaper
11:00							breakfast
12:00	teach	teach	teach	teach	teach		
1:00	lunch	lunch	lunch	lunch	lunch		library
2:00		astronomy lecture			lab work		
3:00				astronomy seminar			
4:00	grocery shopping						
5:00	cook dinner		jog at the beach			jog at the beach	
6:00							
7:00	study	study	study	study			
8:00							

EXERCISE #4. PREPOSITIONS OF TIME. LEVEL A.

Directions Look at Jonathan's schedule. Fill in the blanks with the appropriate preposition:

IN   ON   AT   UNTIL   FROM . . . TO

example _____*On*_____ Monday, Jonathan has breakfast _____*at*_____ seven o'clock.

1. Monday through Friday, Jonathan teaches _____ twelve o'clock.

2. _____ Wednesday and Friday, _____ nine o'clock _____ eleven o'clock, he has his physics discussion section.

3. _____ Wednesday and Saturday _____ the afternoon, he jogs at the beach.

4. He usually teaches _____ noon.

5. _____ the evening _____ weekdays, he usually studies.

6. _____ Tuesday he works on his thesis _____ eleven o'clock.

7. _____ Sunday he's at the library _____ one o'clock.

Name: _____ Date: _____ **237**

8. _____ Sunday _____ the morning he plays tennis with Bill.

9. He works in the lab _____ Friday _____ six o'clock.

10. He always cooks dinner _____ Monday _____ five.

EXERCISE #5. IMPERATIVES. LEVEL A.

Directions Read the situations below. Then choose the correct imperative and write it in the blank.

 example Chrissy wants a hot dog. She needs money. She says to Darlene:

 Please give me some money.
 a. Let's buy a hot dog.   b. Please give me some money.   c. Go get a hot dog.

1. Jonathan is coming home from campus. The front door is locked. He doesn't have his key. Darlene is standing in the living room. He yells to Darlene:

 _____

 a. Open the door.   b. Let's unlock the door.   c. Don't forget your key.

2. Darlene is busy. She is cooking dinner. The garbage can is full. Bill is standing next to the garbage can. She says to Bill:

 _____

 a. Let's take out the trash.   b. Go get the trash.   c. Please take out the trash.

3. Meg's studying for an exam. Bill is playing his stereo loud. Meg can't concentrate. She says to Bill.

 _____

 a. Please turn down your stereo.   b. Let's listen to music.   c. Turn up your stereo.

4. Bill is playing tennis with Jonathan. They're very tired. It's a hot day. They're both very thirsty. He says to Jonathan:

 _____

 a. Don't play tennis.   b. Go get a beer.   c. Let's go get a beer.

5. Darlene and Meg are going shopping. Darlene's car is at the repair shop. She says to Meg:

 _____

 a. Don't take my car.   b. Let's take the bus.   c. Let's go shopping.

6. Bill is cooking dinner. He's making spaghetti. The sauce is burning, and the door bell is ringing. He says to Chrissy:

 _____

 a. Let's make spaghetti.   b. Go answer the door.   c. Don't burn the sauce.

7. Chrissy's finishing her math homework. She needs help with the last problem. Gary's good at math. Chrissy says:

 _____

 a. Let's do my math homework.   b. Go get my math book.   c. Please help me with this problem.

8. Chrissy and Darlene are at the dentist. They're looking at Chrissy's X-rays. Chrissy has six cavities. Darlene asks the dentist for advice. He says to Chrissy:

 _____

 a. Don't eat candy.   b. Let's brush after every meal.   c. Go brush your teeth.

EXERCISE #6. PREPOSITIONS OF PLACE. LEVEL A.

Directions Fill in the blank with the appropriate preposition:

IN	UNDER	UPSTAIRS	IN FRONT (OF)
ON	OVER	DOWNSTAIRS	IN BACK (OF)
AT	BEHIND	ABOVE	

example There's a car ____*in*____ the garage.

The garage is ____*behind*____ the house.

There's a television antenna ____*on*____ the roof.

CHRISSY'S ROOM

1. a. Chrissy's dirty clothes are _____ the bed.

   b. Her shoes are _____ the bed.

   c. There's a picture _____ the wall _____ the bed.

BATHROOM

KITCHEN

2. a. The bathroom is _____ and the kitchen is _____.

   b. Chrissy's toys are _____ the stairs.

   c. There's a picture _____ the stairs.

Name: _____   Date: _____

3. a. Someone is _____ the door.

   b. Darlene is _____ the dining room.

   c. She's sitting _____ the table, and Chrissy is playing _____ the house.

   d. There's a car _____ the house.

Gary's schedule

TIME	MONDAY	TUESDAY	WEDNESDAY	THURSDAY	FRIDAY	SATURDAY	SUNDAY
7:00	breakfast				breakfast		
8:00	teacher's meeting	breakfast	breakfast	breakfast	playground duty		
9:00	teach	teach	teach	teach	teach	breakfast with Adrienne	
10:00						bike riding	
11:00						with Adrienne	brunch with Adrienne
12:00	lunch	lunch	lunch	lunch	lunch		
1:00	teach	teach	teach	teach	teach		
2:00							SAILING
3:00	tennis with Bill	Little League			meet Chrissy		
4:00		Baseball Practice	teacher's meeting	shopping			
5:00				cook dinner			
6:00						dinner with Adrienne	
7:00	prepare class	prepare class	prepare class	prepare class		movies	prepare class
8:00							

240

EXERCISE #7. THE SIMPLE PRESENT TENSE AND PREPOSITIONS OF TIME. LEVEL B.

Directions Look at Gary's schedule on page 240 For each activity below, write a sentence using the present tense. Use the prepositions IN, ON, AT, FROM . . . TO.

example Gary / have a teachers' meeting

Gary has a teachers' meeting on Monday at 8 o'clock in the morning.

1. Gary / meet Chrissy

_____

2. Gary / have playground duty

_____

3. Gary / cook dinner

_____

4. Gary and Adrienne / go to the movies

_____

5. Gary / have brunch with Adrienne

_____

6. Gary and Adrienne / go bike riding

_____

7. Gary / have Little League baseball practice

_____

8. Gary and Bill / play tennis

_____

EXERCISE #8. INTERROGATIVES. LEVEL B.

Directions Read the following dialogue. Using the interrogatives listed below, write Jonathan's mother's questions.

WHERE   WHO   WHEN   HOW MUCH
WHAT   WHOSE   HOW MANY

example *Mother:* Hello.
  Jonathan: Hi.
  Mother: ___*who is it*___?
  Jonathan: It's *me*, Mom. Jonathan.

Mother: Jonathan! How are you, dear?
Jonathan: I'm fine, Mom . . . and you?

242

Mother: I'm fine.

_____?
(1)

Jonathan: I'm at the apartment. I have great news. We have a new place to live.
Mother: That's great, honey.

_____?
(2)

Jonathan: It's in Venice, near the beach.

Mother: _____?
(3)

Jonathan: I'm still living with Gary . . . and we have several other roommates.

Mother: _____?
(4)

Jonathan: The rent's only $850 a month, plus utilities.
Mother: $850!

_____?
(5)

Jonathan: There are five bedrooms, but one is very small.

Mother: _____?
(6)

Jonathan: The small one is Meg's.

Mother: _____?
(7)

Jonathan: She's just a friend.

Mother: _____?
(8)

Jonathan: She's a graduate student.
Mother: Are your other roommates students also?

_____?
(9)

Jonathan: Some of them are part-time students, and one is a tennis teacher.

Mother: _____?
(10)

Jonathan: Bill's the tennis teacher. He's our ex-neighbor.
Mother: That's nice. I'm so glad you finally have a place to live.

_____?
(11)

Jonathan: Classes are beginning next week.

Mother: _____?
(12)

Jonathan: I'm taking four classes.
Mother: Well, that's nice. I hope they're not too hard.
Jonathan: Me too. Oh, by the way . . . get a piece of paper. Here's my new address.
Mother: Wait a minute . . . okay.
Jonathan: It's 1843 Rose Avenue, Los Angeles, California 90291.
Mother: Okay. Call again soon.
Jonathan: Sure, Mom. Talk to you later. Bye, Mom.

Name: _____   Date: _____

EXERCISE #9. IMPERATIVES. LEVEL B.

Directions Look at the following pictures. Write an appropriate command. Use the simple imperative form.

example _make the bed._

1.

   _____

2.

   _____

3.

   _____

4.

   _____

5.
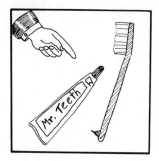

_____

6.
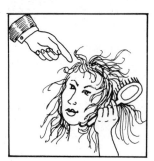

_____

7.

_____

8.

_____

Name: _____ Date: _____

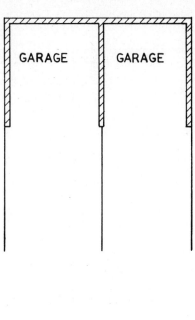

GARAGE   GARAGE

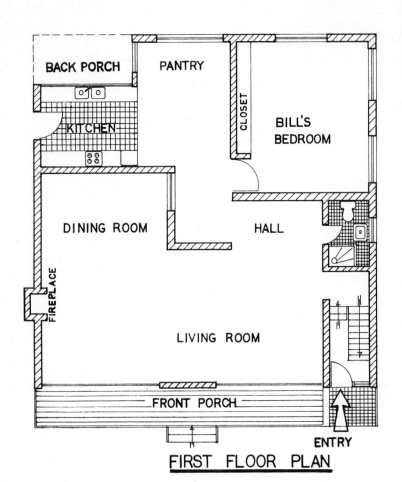

BACK PORCH   PANTRY

CLOSET

BILL'S
BEDROOM

KITCHEN

DINING ROOM

HALL

FIREPLACE

LIVING ROOM

FRONT PORCH

ENTRY

FIRST FLOOR PLAN

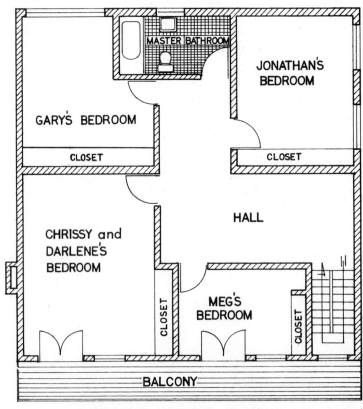

MASTER BATHROOM

JONATHAN'S
BEDROOM

GARY'S BEDROOM

CLOSET

CLOSET

HALL

CHRISSY and
DARLENE'S
BEDROOM

CLOSET

MEG'S
BEDROOM

CLOSET

BALCONY

SECOND FLOOR PLAN

EXERCISE #10. PREPOSITIONS OF PLACE. PART I. LEVEL B.

Directions Look at the floor plan of the house on page 246. Read the descriptions below. In the blank, write the name of the part of the house described.

> **example** It's behind the house, near Bill's bedroom.
> What is it? *It's the garage.*

1. It's opposite Gary's bedroom, next to the bathroom.

   What is it? _____

2. There's a small one on the first floor near the entry and a large one on the second floor.

   What are they? _____

3. It's in the front of the house on the second floor. Meg and Darlene can put their plants on it.

   What is it? _____

4. It's on the first floor below Darlene and Chrissy's room. It's in the front of the house.

   What is it? _____

5. It's upstairs at the end of the hall between Gary's and Jonathan's rooms.

   What is it? _____

6. It's above the kitchen on the second floor.

   What is it? _____

7. It's behind the kitchen.

   What is it? _____

8. There's one on the first floor at the back of the house and there are four on the second floor.

   What are they? _____

EXERCISE #10. PREPOSITIONS OF PLACE. PART II. LEVEL B.

Directions Write one or two sentences describing the location of the given object.

> **example** picture
> a. *There's a picture on the wall.*
> b. *The picture is above the table.*

1. mirror

   a. _____

   b. _____

2. small plant

   a. _____

   b. _____

3. large plant

   a. _____

   b. _____

4. lamp

   a. _____

   b. _____

5. rug

   a. _____

   b. _____

6. stereo

   a. _____

7. books and records

   a. _____

8. logs

   a. _____

9. magazines

   a. _____

10. coffee table

   a. _____

   b. _____

EXERCISE #11. PART I. LEVEL C.

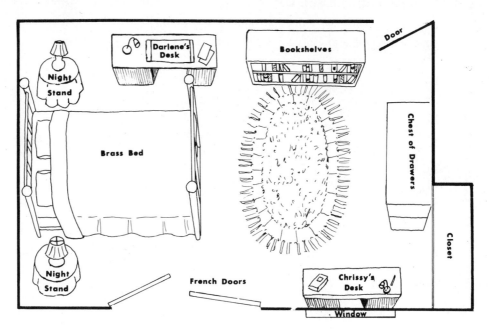

Directions   Read the following dialogue.

Gary: Okay, where can I put this bed?

Darlene: Put it against the wall, over there, and put the nightstands on each side of the bed. Where are the lamps for the nightstands?

Gary: Are they the tall, thin ones or the small, brass ones?

Darlene: They're the brass ones. The tall thin ones go on my desk and on Chrissy's.

Bill: Great, but where can I put the desks?

Chrissy: I want mine in front of the window.

Darlene: Okay, and put mine against the other wall. The book shelves go next to the door.

Gary: And what about the chest of drawers?

Darlene: Oh, we don't have enough space. Let's put it over there, by the closet.

Gary: Okay, I think that's everything now. Here's your rug for the center. Now we're done with your room.

Meg's room

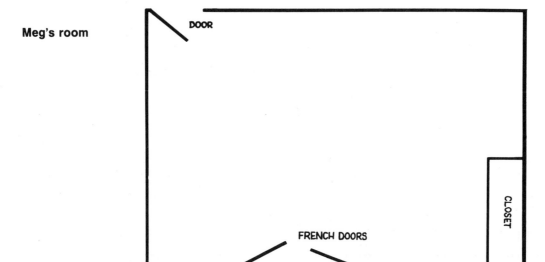

Name: _____   Date: _____   **249**

EXERCISE #11.   PART II.   LEVEL C.

Directions   Look at Meg's room on page 249 and at her things below. Write a dialogue between Meg, Gary, and Bill. Meg is telling Bill and Gary where she wants her things in her room.

These are Meg's things

PEACE CONFERENCE

Darlene:	Let's all sit down and have a conference. We need to make some decisions about our schedules. Chrissy, go call Bill.
Meg:	Yeah, this place is a mess. Chrissy leaves her toys everywhere, and nobody washes the dirty dishes in the sink. We have to divide up the work.
Gary:	I'll do the gardening and take out the trash, but I hate housework, and I can't cook.
Jonathan:	Yeah, he burns everything. I think a woman's place is in the kitchen.
Darlene and Meg:	Wait a minute! What's this??
Darlene:	We like to garden too.
Meg:	And I don't like to cook. Bill makes great spaghetti. Let's have Bill cook dinners.
Bill:	What's happening? What's all the commotion?
Darlene:	We're dividing up the chores. When do you want to wash dishes?
Bill:	Never. I work too hard during the day and I'm really clumsy; I drop dishes. But I like to garden.
Meg:	What about cooking?
Bill:	I can't cook well. I only make spaghetti, but I can take out the trash.
Darlene:	Let's get serious. We have to share the cooking. Let's figure out our schedules so everyone cooks one dinner a week.
Gary:	What about the mornings and afternoons and weekends?
Meg:	Let's only plan for dinners during the week because our schedules are so different. I work Monday and Wednesday in the evening, and I usually go out on Friday. I can cook on Tuesday.

Darlene:	Okay, and I'm home Friday evenings because of Chrissy, so I can cook Friday dinners. Jonathan, when do you have time?
Jonathan:	I guess Monday is okay.
Darlene:	Bill? Gary?
Gary:	On Wednesdays I get home at six o'clock because we have a teachers' meeting every week. Is Thursday okay?
Darlene:	Sure, then Bill has Wednesdays.
Bill:	I guess that's okay.
Meg:	What about grocery shopping? I don't have a car. How do I get to the market from here?
Darlene:	We can shop together. I usually go by car for the weekly shopping, but there's also a small market down the street. You can walk there when I'm not home.
Bill:	What time is it? I'm meeting Susie at 10:30.
Gary:	10:30!! Isn't that a little late??
Bill:	No, she works until 10:00.
Gary:	Well, it's 10:15 now.
Bill:	See you later.

THE SIMPLE PRESENT TENSE: PART II

Chrissy Kids Nobody I My date Bill		leaves ask washes hate works makes	her toys everywhere. a lot of questions. the dirty dishes. homework. until ten o'clock. really great spaghetti.	
Do Does Do Does	you Bill they Darlene		have want like have to	time on Wednesday? to wash dishes? to garden? stay home on Friday?	Yes, I do. No, he doesn't. Yes, they do. Yes, she does.
Don't Doesn't Doesn't Don't	you Meg Bill they		like have have wash	to garden? a car? a date? their dishes?	Yes, I do. No, she doesn't. Yes, he does. No, they don't.
	Meg Darlene I They	doesn't doesn't don't don't	work go out have plan	on Tuesday. on Friday. a car. dinners on the weekends.	

Notes

A. Use the simple present tense to talk about a habitual activity. (See Chapters Nine and Eleven.)

B. Questions: The auxiliary DO/DOES or a contraction of DO/DOES plus NOT comes before the subject.

$$\left\{ {DO \atop DOES} \right\} + (NOT) + \underline{\hphantom{xxxx}}_{(subject)} + \underline{\hphantom{xx}}_{(verb)}$$

examples   Do you have time on Wednesday?
Does Bill wash the dishes?
Doesn't Bill have a date?
Don't you have a car?

C. Responses
1. Use DO(N'T) and DOES(N'T) with short answers. (See Chapter Eight.)

   examples   Do you have a car?
   No, I don't.
   Doesn't he make good spaghetti?
   Yes, he does.

2. You can give additional information after the YES or NO answer.

   examples   Doesn't Jonathan have a motorcycle?
   Yes, he has a Suzuki 350.
   Do you drive to school?
   No, I take the bus.

D. Negative statements: The auxiliaries DON'T and DOESN'T come before the base form of the verb.

$$\underline{\qquad} \; + \; \begin{Bmatrix} \text{DON'T} \\ \text{DOESN'T} \end{Bmatrix} \; + \; \underline{\qquad}$$
$$\text{(subject)} \qquad\qquad\qquad \text{(base form of} \\ \text{the verb)}$$

examples   I don't have a car.
Meg doesn't work on Tuesdays.

NEED AND *WANT:* PART II

Chrissy wants a new bicycle.
Meg needs a car.
Bill wants more tennis students.
We need to make some decisions about our schedules.
Darlene needs to find a babysitter.
When do you want to wash dishes?

Notes

A. The verbs NEED and WANT take an object.

   examples   Darlene needs *a haircut.*
   (object)
   Meg wants *a new car.*
   (object)

1. NEED and WANT can take a noun object or a verb object.

   examples   I need *a new coat.*
   (noun object)
   Gary wants *to take a vacation.*
   (verb object)

   a. The verb object with NEED and WANT is TO plus the base form of the verb.

$$\begin{Bmatrix} \text{NEED} \\ \text{WANT} \end{Bmatrix} \; + \; \text{TO} \; + \; \underline{\qquad}$$
$$\text{(base form of} \\ \text{the verb)}$$

SUBJECT	VERB	NOUN OBJECT
Bill	wants	more students.
Darlene	needs	a babysitter for Chrissy.
They	need	a large house.

SUBJECT	VERB	VERB OBJECT
Bill	wants	to play tennis.
Chrissy	wants	to watch television.
They	need	to live near campus.

B. Use NEED and WANT in the simple present tense when you are talking about the present time.

examples   Chrissy *wants* to have dinner now.
                Darlene *needs* to go grocery shopping.

HOW?

How do you make spaghetti?
    Take boiling water and add the spaghetti, then . . .
How do you get to work?
    I go by car.
How is your astronomy class?
    It's interesting, but difficult.
How are you?
    I'm fine.
How do I get to the post office from here?
    Go three blocks and turn left at the stop light.
    It's in the middle of the block.

Notes

A. Meaning
  1. Use HOW to ask about someone's health or about a condition.

      examples   How's Dad?
                     He's fine.
                How's the weather?
                     It's cold.

  2. HOW asks about the manner or method of transportation, especially with the verbs GO and GET.

      examples   How does Chrissy go to school?
                     She walks.
                How does Meg get to work?
                     She goes by bus.

  3. HOW asks for instructions.

      examples   How do you make spaghetti?
                     Take boiling water . . .
                How do you change a tire?
                     Open your trunk, take out the jack, and . . .

  4. HOW asks for directions.

      examples   How do I get to the drugstore?
                     Go to the corner and turn right . . .
                How can we get to the beach from here?
                     Go straight down Rose Ave . . .

  5. HOW before certain adjectives asks about a quantity or measurement.

      examples   How tall is Gary?
                     He's 6'2".
                How warm is it today?
                     It's 102 degrees.

6. HOW asks about the manner or method of doing something.

examples   How do you eat Chinese food?
  With chopsticks.
  How are you sending the package?
  Air mail, special delivery.

7. In spoken English the expression HOW COME means WHY.

examples   How come you're so tired?
  I'm not getting enough sleep.
  I'm not staying home tonight.
  How come?
  Because I have a date.

8. HOW asks for the mode of transportation.

examples   How does Chrissy get to school?
  She walks or rides her bike.
  How does Meg get to work?
  She takes the bus.

B. Position: HOW comes at the beginning of information questions. Notice the similarity with YES/NO question word order.

examples   How ⎡ Are you okay?
     ⎣ are you?

    How ⎡ Does Meg get to work by car?
     ⎣ does Meg get to work?

ADVERBS OF MANNER

Chrissy does poorly in school because she never listens.
Bill plays tennis well.
Darlene drives her car too fast.
Bill doesn't wash the dishes carefully; he always drops them.

Notes

A. Use: Adverbs of manner describe an action.

examples   I'm sorry. I can't understand you. You*'re speaking* too *softly*.
  (action)   (adverb)
  Jonathan's always in a hurry, so he *eats*   *quickly*.
  (action) (adverb)

1. Adverbs of manner sometimes answer questions with HOW.

examples   *How* does Chrissy walk to school?
  She walks *slowly*.
  How does she walk home from school?
  She walks *quickly*.

B. Form
  1. Many adverbs of manner have -LY endings. Add -LY to the adjective.

examples   Darlene always speaks *clearly* to Chrissy.
  Meg likes to play her radio *softly* in the evening.

  2. Some adverbs do not have an -LY ending. Their form is the same as the adjective form.

examples   Gary plays his stereo too *loud*.
  Bill works *hard;* he teaches tennis all day.
  Darlene drives her car too *fast*.

3. The adverb WELL is irregular. It corresponds to the adjective GOOD.

> **examples**   Bill is a *good* tennis player.   Meg is not a *good* cook.
> Bill plays tennis *well*.   Meg doesn't cook *well*.

GET

Let's get to work.
On Wednesdays I get home at six.
How do I get to the market from here?
I'm getting a headache.
When are you getting your pay check?

Notes

A. Meaning
  1. GET sometimes means BECOME. It shows a change.

> **examples**   Mr. Garvey is getting old.
> Jonathan jogs because he doesn't want to get fat.
> Meg's sister is getting married.
> Darlene's brother is getting divorced.

  2. GET sometimes means RECEIVE or EARN.

> **examples**   We can get all the old movies on cable television.
> Darlene drives too fast, so she gets speeding tickets.
> Chrissy doesn't get good grades.
> Meg gets $5.65 an hour at work.

  3. GET sometimes means ARRIVE or GO.

> **examples**   Gary gets home late on Wednesdays.
> Chrissy gets to school by nine.

  4. GET is often used in questions with HOW to ask about direction or mode of transportation.

> **examples**   How do you get to work?
>   I go *by bus*.
>   (mode of transportation)
>   How do I get to the bus stop?
>   *Turn left at the corner.*
>   (direction)

  5. GET is used in many idiomatic expressions.

GET ALONG WITH	Bill gets along well with everyone.
	Meg is easy to get along with.
GET ON _____'S NERVES	Meg doesn't like Chrissy; Chrissy
(someone)	gets on her nerves.
	This traffic is getting on my nerves.
GET UP	Darlene has to get up at six o'clock.
	I hate to get up in the morning.
GET TO KNOW	It's nice to get to know you.
	Chrissy wants to get to know the kids
	on her block.
GET THROUGH	Jonathan gets through with his classes
(=to finish)	in the early afternoon.
	I hope I can get through the day.

SO

Bill hates to cook, so he always eats in restaurants.
Chrissy leaves her toys all over her room, so it's a mess.
We have to share the cooking, so everyone cooks one dinner a week.

Notes

A. SO connects two sentences.
1. Use a comma before the conjunction SO.

> **example**   We have to share the cooking.
> Everyone cooks one dinner a week.
>
> ➤We have to share the cooking, *so* everyone cooks one dinner a week.

B. SO combines a reason and a result. SO introduces the result.

> **example**   reason: Chrissy leaves her toys all over her room.
> result: Her room is a mess.
>
> ➤Chrissy leaves her toys all over her room, *so* her room is a mess.

C. Use a pronoun in place of the identical noun in the second part of the sentence.

> **example**   Bill hates to cook.
> Bill always eats in restaurants.
>
> ➤*Bill* hates to cook, so *he* always eats in restaurants.
> (Bill)

BECAUSE OF

Darlene has to be home on Fridays because of Chrissy.
Gary has to be at school early on Mondays because of the teachers' meeting.
Gary comes home late on Tuesday because of Little League.
They like Venice because of the beach.

Notes

A. The preposition BECAUSE OF connects a statement with a noun phrase.

> **examples**   *Darlene has to be home on Fridays* because of *Chrissy.*
> (statement)   (noun phrase)
> *Meg doesn't want to take the bus today* because of *the rain.*
> (statement)   (noun phrase)

B. BECAUSE OF introduces a reason.

> **examples**   Darlene has to be home on Fridays *because of* Chrissy. (Because she has to be home with Chrissy.)
>
> Gary has to be at school early on Mondays *because of* the teachers' meeting. (Because he has to attend a teachers' meeting.)
>
> They like Venice *because of* the beach. (Because they like the beach.)
>
> Gary comes home late on Tuesday *because of* Little League. (Because he supervises Little League.)

Family relationships

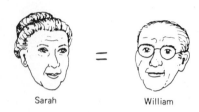

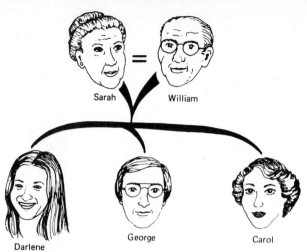

Sarah and William are married.
Sarah is William's *wife*.
William is Sarah's *husband*.

Sarah and William have three *children*.
They have one *son*, George.
They have two *daughters*, Darlene and Carol.

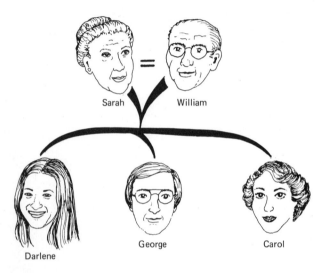

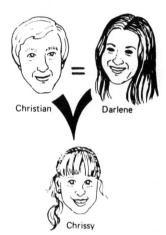

Darlene's *parents* are Sarah and William.
Sarah is Darlene's *mother*.
William is Darlene's *father*.
Darlene has one *brother*, George, and one *sister*, Carol.

Darlene is Chrissy's *mother*.
Christian is Chrissy's *father*.
Christian and Darlene are Chrissy's *parents*.
Chrissy is Christian and Darlene's *daughter*.

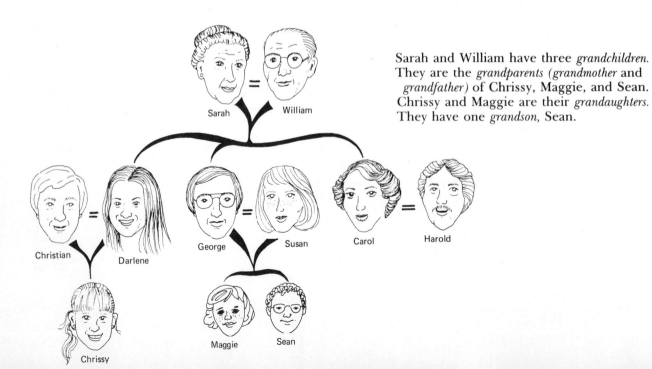

Sarah and William have three *grandchildren*.
They are the *grandparents (grandmother* and
grandfather) of Chrissy, Maggie, and Sean.
Chrissy and Maggie are their *grandaughters*.
They have one *grandson*, Sean.

EXERCISE #1. THE SIMPLE PRESENT TENSE. LEVEL A.

Directions Fill in the blanks with the correct form of the present tense. Use DO or DOES when necessary.

example *Meg:* This place ____*is*____ a mess.
BE

Darlene: You '*re* ____ right. ____*Do*____n't the men

BE

ever ____*Clean up*____ anything?
CLEAN UP

Meg: This _____ terrible. There _____ always newspapers all over the
(1) BE   (2) BE
living room.

Darlene: Yeah, I _____. Bill always _____ his beer cans everywhere.
(3) KNOW   (4) LEAVE

Meg: . . . and the kitchen _____ filthy because Bill never _____ the
(5) BE   (6) DO
dishes when it _____ his turn.
(7) BE

Darlene: But Gary and Jonathan _____ cooperative. They _____ to
(8) BE   (9) TRY
keep the place clean.

Meg: That _____ true. Gary _____ and _____
(10) BE   (11) VACUUM   (12) DUST
occasionally, and Jonathan always _____ the trash.
(13) CARRY OUT

Darlene: But that _____ not enough. They _____ things all over the
(14) BE   (15) LEAVE
house.

Name: _____ Date: _____

Meg: Yeah, just like Chrissy! She _____ her toys everywhere.
                                        (16) LEAVE

Darlene: She _____ to pick up her things. She _____ just a kid.
                      (17) TRY   (18) BE

Meg: I _____, but it _____ hard to live in this mess.
              (19) KNOW   (20) BE

Darlene: We _____ a plan. We _____ divide up the chores.
                    (21) NEED   (22) HAVE TO

Meg: But I _____n't _____ housework.
                              (23) LIKE

Darlene: I _____ housework too, but we _____ keep this place clean.
                  (24) HATE   (25) HAVE TO

Meg: I _____ a great idea. The men can do the housework.
              (26) HAVE

Darlene: Great idea . . . and you and I can do the cooking.

Meg: I _____ to cook, too.
              (27) HATE

Darlene: Bill _____ good spaghetti. _____ you _____
                    (28) MAKE   (29) LIKE
spaghetti?

Meg: Sure, I _____ spaghetti, but not every night. _____ he
                  (30) LOVE

_____ anything else?
    (31) MAKE

Darlene: I _____ n't _____. He _____ n't
                  (32) KNOW

_____ very often.
    (33) COOK

Meg: What about Jonathan and Gary?

Darlene: I _____ Gary _____ every day until five, so he can't cook dinner.
                  (34) THINK   (35) WORK

He can do the dishes, though. And Jonathan _____ free after 5 o'clock every
                                                          (36) BE

day. He _____n't _____ any classes in the evening.
                              (37) HAVE

Meg: Let's talk about this at dinner tonight.

Darlene: Okay. By the way, when do you leave in the morning?

Meg: I _____ at 8:30 every morning. I _____ be at work at 9:00.
              (38) LEAVE   (39) HAVE TO

Darlene: Chrissy _____ at 8:30 also. Can you watch her tomorrow?
                      (40) LEAVE

I _____ a dental appointment at 8:00.
      (41) HAVE

Meg: Sure.

Darlene: She _____ breakfast before she _____ to school. Don't let her
        (42) NEED   (43) GO
go without it.

Meg: _____ she _____ to school alone?
                          (44) WALK

Darlene: No, she _____ her friend, Timmy, and they _____ to school
                  (45) MEET   (46) WALK
together.

Meg: Okay, fine.

EXERCISE #2. *WANT/NEED.* LEVEL A.

Directions   Combine the following words to form a sentence.

examples   Bill / want / have / a beer
            Bill wants to have a beer.
            Darlene / need / a babysitter
            Darlene needs a babysitter.

1. Gary / want / fix / his car

   _____

2. Chrissy / want / get / a ten-speed bike

   _____

3. Jonathan / need / a haircut

   _____

4. Bill / want / new stereo speakers

   _____

5. Gary / need / prepare / his lessons

   _____

6. Darlene and Meg / want / take / a vacation

   _____

7. Darlene's car / need / a tune-up

   _____

8. Meg / want / buy / a car

   _____

9. Gary and Adrienne / want / see / a movie

   _____

10. Jonathan and Gary / need / gain / weight

    _____

11. Darlene / want / a better job

    _____

12. Meg / want / get / a master's degree

    _____

Name: _____   Date: _____

EXERCISE #3. INTERROGATIVES. LEVEL A.

Directions Fill in the blank with the correct interrogative from the list below.

HOW   HOW MUCH   WHAT   WHEN
WHO   HOW MANY   WHERE

example *Darlene:* I want to make a phone call. ____*Where*____ is there a pay phone?
            Meg: I think there's one on the corner, in front of the market.

Darlene: Hello, operator? I would like to make a long distance collect call to Tamaqua, Pennsylvania.

Operator: Is this person-to-person or station-to-station?

Darlene: Station-to-station, please.

Operator: _____ number are you calling?
                      (1)

Darlene: The number is 724-8361.

Operator: _____'s the area code for Tamaqua?
                      (2)

Darlene: I think it's 821.

Operator: And _____'s your number?
                      (3)

Darlene: The number here is 625-4321.

Operator: Thank you. I'll put your call through.

                      * * *

Operator: Will you accept a collect call from Los Angeles?

Father: _____'s calling?
                      (4)

Operator: I'm sorry, ma'am. _____'s your name?
                      (5)

262

Darlene:	Daddy, it's me—Darlene.
Father:	Oh, I accept the call. Hi, Darlene.
Operator:	Okay, go ahead.
Darlene:	Hi, Daddy. _____ are you and Mom? (6)
Father:	We're fine. _____'s Chrissy? (7)
Darlene:	She's fine, too.
Father:	_____ are you calling from? Do you have a phone? (8)
Darlene:	Not yet, I'm calling from a pay phone. We have a house but there's no phone yet.
Father:	That's great, but can you afford a house? _____ is the rent? (9)
Darlene:	The rent is $850, but I have some roommates.
Father:	_____ are your roommates? (10)
Darlene:	Just some friends. Do you remember Meg? She's living with us.
Father:	Sure, I remember Meg. Well, that's nice. _____ is your house? Is it close to (11) campus?
Darlene:	It's in Venice. It's about 20 minutes by car to campus.
Father:	_____'s Venice like? (12)
Darlene:	It's an old neighborhood near the beach.
Father:	Oh, here's your mother. I'll let you talk to her.
Mother:	Hi, Darlene. _____ are you coming to visit us? We miss you. (13)
Darlene:	Maybe at Christmas. I'm not sure, but Chrissy and I both have vacations at Christmas. Mother, we have a house.
Mother:	Great, _____ did you move in? (14)
Darlene:	Friday was moving day.
Mother:	Is it a big house? _____ bedrooms are there? (15)
Darlene:	It's a five-bedroom house.
Mother:	Five bedrooms!! Do you need such a big house?
Darlene:	Well, I have four roommates. You remember Meg? She's living with us.
Mother:	_____ are the rooms like? (16)
Darlene:	They're big with high ceilings, and two bedrooms open onto a balcony. Chrissy and I are sharing so we have the master bedroom. It's one of the rooms with the balcony, so it gets a lot of light.
Mother:	Are you still working?

Name: _____   Date: _____

Darlene: Yes, but only part-time.

Mother: _____ days a week do you work?
                    (17)

Darlene: I work two days, Tuesday and Thursday. Mom, I'll call you again when we get our phone. This is an expensive call.

Mother: Wait, _____ is your new address?
                    (18)

Darlene: I'll send it to you.

Mother: Okay, call again soon. We want to hear about your new house.

Darlene: Bye, Mom. Say goodbye to Dad.

Mother: Okay. Bye, Darlene.

EXERCISE #4.   ADVERBS OF MANNER.   LEVEL A.

Directions   Fill in the blank with the appropriate adverb of manner.

   example   Darlene gets many speeding tickets; she drives too *fast*_____.
                    a. carefully   b. hard   c. fast

1. I can't understand you. You're speaking too fast. Please speak _____.
   a. quickly   b. slowly   c. fast

2. Chrissy likes to chew bubble gum. No one can understand her because she doesn't

   speak _____ with bubble gum in her mouth.
   a. clearly   b. softly   c. slowly

3. Bill's a tennis teacher. He plays tennis very _____.
   a. poorly   b. clearly   c. well

4. Gary likes to play his radio very _____ at night, and Chrissy can't sleep.
   a. softly   b. loud   c. carefully

5. Meg likes quiet music when she studies, so she plays the radio _____.
   a. loud   b. softly   c. clearly

6. Mr. Garvey's a little deaf. You have to speak _____ so he can hear you.
   a. fast   b. loud   c. hard

7. Chrissy doesn't get good grades. She does _____ in school.
   a. well   b. carefully   c. poorly

8. Chrissy usually has her dinner at 5:45. She has to eat _____ because her favorite
   a. quickly   b. slowly   c. carefully

   television program is on at 6:00.

9. Darlene never has car accidents. She drives very _____.
   a. poorly   b. clearly   c. carefully

10. Jonathan does _____ in school because he studies all the time.
    a. hard   b. well   c. poorly

EXERCISE #5.   *BECAUSE/BECAUSE OF/SO.*   LEVEL A.

Directions   Fill in the blanks with:

                    BECAUSE   BECAUSE OF   SO
Use a comma when necessary.

examples 1. I can't cook _____*so*_____ I always burn everything.

2. Gary can't prepare dinner on Thursday _*because of*_ the teachers' meeting.

3. Bill eats in restaurants _*because*_ he hates to cook.

1. Jonathan studies very hard _____ he gets good grades.

2. Chrissy leaves early for school _____ she has to walk.

3. Jonathan is in good condition _____ he jogs at the beach.

4. We're not playing tennis today _____ the rain.

5. Jonathan teaches at twelve o'clock _____ he can't have lunch until one.

6. Meg doesn't like Chrissy _____ she's nosy.

7. Gary doesn't teach school on Saturday _____ he sleeps late.

8. We're never all at home together _____ our schedules.

9. The market is only a block away _____ we can walk there.

10. Meg gets home late _____ her job.

EXERCISE #6. FAMILY RELATIONSHIPS. PART I. LEVEL A.

Directions Fill in the blanks with the name of the appropriate person.

example _*George*_ is Maggie's father.

1. George's wife is _____ and his children are _____
and _____.

2. George is the son of _____ and _____ and the brother of
_____ and _____.

Name: _____ Date: _____

3. _____ and _____ are George's parents. _____ is his

mother and _____ is his father.

4. _____ and _____ are George's sisters.

5. _____ is Susan's husband.

EXERCISE #6. FAMILY RELATIONSHIPS. PART II. LEVEL A.

Directions Look at Darlene's family on page 265. Fill in the blanks below with the name of the appropriate family relationship.

    example Darlene is Chrissy's _mother_.

1. Chrissy's _____ are Sarah and William.

2. Chrissy's _____ is William and her _____ is Sarah.

3. Chrissy is Sarah and William's _____.

4. Chrissy, Maggie, and Sean are the _____ of Sarah and William.

5. Sean is Sarah and William's _____.

6. Darlene and Carol are Sarah and William's _____.

EXERCISE #7. *WANT/NEED.* LEVEL B.

Directions For each situation below, write two sentences.
           a. Use WANT or NEED and a noun object.
           b. Use WANT or NEED and a verb object.

    example Darlene has a date Friday evening. She can't leave Chrissy alone.
        a. _She needs a babysitter._
        b. _She needs to get a babysitter._

1. Meg's hair is too long.

    a. _____

    b. _____

2. Jonathan doesn't have any money. He has to go grocery shopping.

    a. _____

    b. _____

3. Darlene has a flat tire.

    a. _____

    b. _____

4. Bill's thirsty.

    a. _____

    b. _____

5. Meg has a headache.

    a. _____

    b. _____

6. Darlene is poor. She can't pay her bills.

    a. _____

    b. _____

7. Darlene and Meg are hungry.

    a. _____

    b. _____

8. Chrissy is lonely because she's new in school.

    a. _____

    b. _____

EXERCISE #8. INTERROGATIVES. LEVEL B.

Directions Read the following short dialogues. Then write the appropriate question in the blank.

    examples *Meg:* *Whose turn is it to do the dishes?*
                 Darlene: It's Bill's turn to do the dishes.

                 Meg: *Where is he* ?
                 Darlene: He's at Donkin's Bar.

1. *Chrissy:* Mom, _____?
                                    (a)

    Darlene: It's four-thirty.

    Chrissy: I'm hungry. _____?
                                    (b)

    Darlene: Dinner is at five.

    Chrissy: _____?
                                    (c)

    Darlene: Bill's cooking dinner.

    Chrissy: _____?
                                    (d)

    Darlene: We're having spaghetti.

2. *Tennis student:* I want to learn to play tennis.

    Bill: Okay. Do you want private or group lessons?

    Student: _____?
                                    (a)

    Bill: Private lessons are $20 an hour.

    Student: _____?
                                    (b)

    Bill: Group lessons are $7 an hour.

    Student: I think I want group lessons.

    _____?
                                    (c)

    Bill: They're on Saturday mornings from nine to two.

Name: _____ Date: _____

Student:	_____ ? (d)
Bill:	The courts are in the Marina. We play at the Hyatt Courts on Lincoln Blvd.

3. *Gary:*   Chrissy, how was your first day at school?

   Chrissy: Oh, it was okay, but I don't know anyone.

   Gary: _____ ?

(a)

   Chrissy: My teacher? He's nice, but I think he's too strict.

   Gary: _____ ?

(b)

   Chrissy: His name is Mr. Wong.

   Gary: _____ ?

(c)

   Chrissy: Oh, I guess about 30 kids are in the class.

   Gary: _____ ?

(d)

   Chrissy: We're in room 34.

EXERCISE #9. *BECAUSE/SO.* LEVEL B.

Directions   Combine the two sentences with SO or BECAUSE. When there are two sentences with identical nouns, use a pronoun in place of the second noun.

    example   Chrissy's house is close to school.
                   Chrissy walks to school.
       Chrissy's house is close to school, so she walks there.

1. Adrienne is angry with Gary.
   Gary is always late.

_____

_____

2. Meg's bus is very slow.
   Meg is often late for work.

_____

_____

3. Gary has a teachers' meeting early Monday morning.
   Gary wants to go to sleep early Sunday evening.

_____

_____

4. Bill has a very busy life.
   Bill has many girl friends.

_____

_____

5. Bill can only cook spaghetti.
   Bill cooks spaghetti every Thursday.

   _____

   _____

6. Meg goes out every Friday.
   Meg is never at home Friday evenings.

   _____

   _____

7. Darlene and Chrissy share a room.
   Darlene and Chrissy have the big bedroom.

   _____

   _____

8. Darlene likes the neighborhood.
   The neighborhood is safe.

   _____

   _____

EXERCISE #10.   FAMILY RELATIONSHIPS.   LEVEL B.

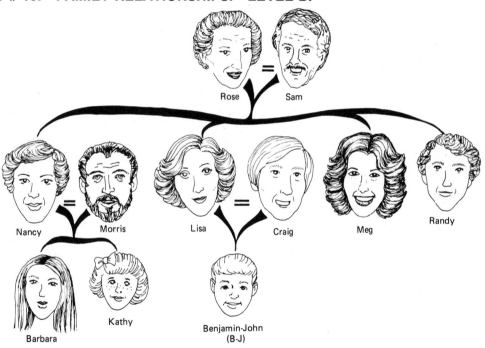

Directions   Write two sentences showing the relationship between the two people.

example   Meg / Rose a. _Meg is Rose's daughter._
               b. _Rose is Meg's mother._

1. Randy / Sam

   a. _____

   b. _____

Name: _____   Date: _____

2. Nancy / Barbara

    a. _____

    b. _____

3. Lisa / Craig

    a. _____

    b. _____

4. Lisa and Craig / B-J

    a. _____

    b. _____

5. Meg and Randy / Rose

    a. _____

    b. _____

6. Nancy / Randy

    a. _____

    b. _____

7. Barbara, Kathy, B-J / Rose

    a. _____

       _____

    b. _____

       _____

8. B-J / Rose and Sam

    a. _____

    b. _____

9. Barbara / Sam

    a. _____

    b. _____

10. Morris / Kathy

    a. _____

    b. _____

EXERCISE #11. PART I. LEVEL C.

Directions Look at Jonathan's weekly schedule on page 237. Then read the model paragraph below.

Jonathan is a serious student. He works hard. He gets up early every day because he doesn't like to sleep late, and he has breakfast at 7 o'clock. He gets to the university at 7:50 because he likes to start his day early. He studies physics and astronomy, and he has a part-time job. He teaches every day at noon, Monday through Friday. Every Wednesday and Friday morning he has a physics discussion section with his students. His physics lab is on Monday from 8 to 12, and he does lab work on Friday from 2 to 6. His astronomy classes are on Tuesday and Thursday in the afternoon. Jonathan isn't athletic, but he doesn't want to get fat, so he jogs at the beach on Wednesday and Saturday in the late afternoon. He also plays tennis with Bill on Sunday mornings. He is always very busy.

Name: _____   Date: _____   271

EXERCISE #11. PART II. LEVEL C.

Directions Look at Meg's daily schedule. Write a paragraph describing her activities.

Meg's daily schedule

TIME	MONDAY	TUESDAY	WEDNESDAY	THURSDAY	FRIDAY	SATURDAY	SUNDAY
7:00		jog at the beach		jog at the beach			
8:00	Management class		Management class		Management class		Tennis with Darlene
9:00	↓		↓		↓		↓
10:00	Business law	Accounting class	Business law	Accounting class		jog?	brunch
11:00	↓	↓	↓	↓		brunch	
12:00	lunch	lunch	lunch	lunch	lunch		
1:00	study in		study in	WORK			beach? sailing?
2:00	the library		the library			go shopping	bike ride?
3:00		go grocery shopping	↓		Data processing class		
4:00	dinner		dinner	↓	↓	↓	
5:00	WORK	cook dinner	WORK				↓
6:00						dinner with Christopher	
7:00		Rehearse with		ice skating lesson	date with Burt		study?
8:00	↓	theater group	↓	↓	↓	movies	

_____

_____

_____

_____

_____

_____

_____

_____

_____

_____
_____
_____
_____
_____
_____
_____
_____

EXERCISE #11. PART III. LEVEL C.

Directions Fill in **Your daily schedule** with your daily activities. Write a paragraph describing your daily activities.

Your daily schedule

TIME	MONDAY	TUESDAY	WEDNESDAY	THURSDAY	FRIDAY	SATURDAY	SUNDAY
7:00							
8:00							
9:00							
10:00							
11:00							
12:00							
1:00							
2:00							
3:00							
4:00							
5:00							
6:00							
7:00							
8:00							

Name: _____ Date: _____

Your paragraph

INDEX